30 BREADS TO BAKE

Before You Die

THE WORLD'S BEST SOURDOUGH, CROISSANTS, FOCACCIA, BAGELS, PITA, AND MORE FROM YOUR FAVORITE BAKERS (INCLUDING DOMINIQUE ANSEL, DUFF GOLDMAN, AND DEB PERELMAN)

BY ALLYSON REEDY

Select photography by Vanessa Mir

Published by:
Ulysses Press
PO Box 3440
Berkeley, CA 94703
www.ulyssespress.com

ISBN: 978-1-64604-679-9
Library of Congress Control Number: 2024931671

Printed in China
10 9 8 7 6 5 4 3 2 1

Acquisitions editor: Kierra Sondereker
Managing editor: Claire Chun
Editor: Renee Rutledge
Front cover and interior design: Raquel Castro
Layout: Winnie Liu
Interior photography: Vanessa Mir except page 57 © Evan Sung; page 64 © Arturo Enciso; page 68 © Kimberly
   Yang; page 79 © Ana Frias; page 85 © Casey Wilson; page 104 © Sam Hanna

Like everything, this book is dedicated to my two little taste testers (and the one bigger taste tester) who make up 99% of my happiness. Carbs take care of the rest.

CONTENTS

INTRODUCTION

Making and baking bread in our instant-gratification culture is almost revolutionary, a coup against the temptation to take shortcuts to get what you want *right now*. Making bread takes our most precious resource of all—time. But it turns that time into fluffy Hokkaido milk bread and crusty smoked oat sourdough, so I'd say it's time well spent.

The quickest recipe in this book takes 30 minutes—a jiffy compared to the three-day-long process of making a demi-baguette (eight days if you count the time to create its starter)—but most recipes take several hours, if not a couple of days. So yeah, you're downright rebelling against the now in favor of the later, you radical, you.

Here's what you already know, or what you're about to know: It's worth it. It's worth waiting for the flour's friendly bacteria to pop up and say hello, for the yeast to get nice and bubbly, for the dough to truly double in size, and for your loaf to fully cool and set before slicing. (Okay maybe that last one is asking too much.)

The time it takes to make bread is both a beautiful thing and a challenging thing. But you fellow carb mutineers are here for the challenge. You are here for the sourdoughs, the wheats, and the rolls. The croissants, the pitas, the biscuits, the bagels. And let's not forget the sweetest breads of all: the cinnamon rolls, the babka king cakes, the banana breads, and Lord help us, the chocolate chip brioche.

You are a bread lover in all of its glorious forms, and you are now on a fluffy, crusty collision course with the best bread of your life.

Who Needs This Book?

This book is written for people who are intimidated by the word "starter," and who think levain is just a bakery that makes really good cookies. People who really, really love bread, but who may not know exactly where to start when it comes to baking it themselves. People like me.

I'm learning right along with you. I'm a restaurant critic and food writer, but my bread baking skills are probably right about where yours are. This is my first time mixing together water and flour and expecting magic (which is to say, my first time making my own sourdough starter), but luckily the experts who gave us these recipes know what they're doing. We're in good hands with their tested, dialed-in recipes—and I'm here to translate their weird bread-baking jargon like "autolyze" into understandable terms.

The recipes, tips, and tricks in this book come from expert dough workers and bread magicians. They've put in the hours of kneading, proofing, stretching, folding, and baking to perfect these recipes, all in the oh-so-noble name of good bread. Our job is to simply show up in the kitchen, get our hands dirty, and be willing to mess up. Because even the most disastrous bread mess-ups are still going to taste pretty darn good.

How to Use This Book

Whether you start with a longer sourdough recipe or a quick banana bread to build your confidence is up to you, but please keep one thing in mind: everything can be fussy. From the state of your starter to how your dough comes together in your kitchen's dry or humid air to how aggressive you are with the stretch and folds to your feelings about Taylor Swift. All fussy.

At times you may have to use your best judgment and add a little extra liquid (just a little!) if the dough isn't coming together. You may need to refresh your baking powder and yeast, because they aren't meant to last the duration of a presidency. You might, like I did, screw up the shaping of your baguette on your first go and decide to either call it or start over again in an attempt to make that baguette your b!tch.

Above all, you must approach this book with grace—*for yourself*. You've accomplished something just by showing up in the kitchen, probably with flour all over your face, and kneading your way to something that's going to taste great. Even if your baguette is a little wonky.

But First, a Couple of Things

Some bread recipes take very little in terms of time, ingredients, and effort. And others… not so much. It's important to know whether you're getting into an hour-long, start-to-finish project or a loaf that takes a couple of days. (Plus more if you need to get your starter going.) So read the recipe before you tackle it. You'll know what to expect, and you'll be in the best possible position for success.

You'll notice that some recipes use cup measurements, while others use grams. (And some use both!) These recipes were gifted to us by the best bakers around, so instead of trying to translate to a less accurate, standardized format, I decided to stick with the recipe creators' intentions. Their recipes, as they wrote them, will perform best for you, whether that means you scoop flour into a cup or weigh it using a kitchen scale. Which brings us to another point…

You Need a Kitchen Scale

For the most precise, consistent-results-every-time breads, you have to use a kitchen scale. My cup of flour and yours could be off by several grams. (Is it scooped and leveled? Heaping? Packed?) By weighing each ingredient, you know you've got the proper amount.

There are SO Many Different Types of Flours

What's the difference between all-purpose and OO, and what the heck is bread flour anyway? The good news is that some flours can easily be swapped for one another, meaning if you can't find tapioca flour, you'll be okay using the rice flour that's already in your pantry. Higher protein flours like bread (made from hard wheat with lots of protein), all-purpose, and whole wheat strengthen gluten production, while lower-protein flours like cake and pastry make for a more delicate crumb.

You Might Have to Do Math Via Baker's Percentages

Bakers have a quasi-language all their own, called baker's percentages. The purpose is to precisely scale a recipe up or down—just in case you want to make baguettes for the neighborhood or you have a major cinnamon roll craving.

The main thing you need to know about baker's percentages is that the flour weight is always 100%, and all other ingredients are expressed as a percentage of the flour. Here's an example:

Ingredients	Weight	Baker's Percentage
Flour	450 grams	100%
Water	250 grams	55.5%
Salt	8 grams	2%
Yeast	5 grams	1%

The equation is the ingredient/flour x 100. So, for water, this would be 250/450 x 100 = 55.5%. You don't need to get out your calculator to make the recipes in this book, but if you'd like to change up the quantities, this is a helpful tool to know.

For a Lot of Recipes, You Need a Starter

It's tempting to skip the recipes that require a sourdough starter. (That's what I would have done!) But getting a starter going and keeping it alive doesn't have to be a production. I mean, it can be. (Some bread people are, well, *interesting*.) But it doesn't have to be. The guide on page 11 will get you going, and then guess what? After you're done using it, you can just stick it in the fridge and it'll wait oh so patiently until you pull it out to make another loaf.

If you want to bake fresh bread every day for the rest of your life, great! Leave that baby on your countertop and feed it twice a day. But if sourdough is more of an occasional thing in your household, I don't want you to think that having a starter means never getting a sick day or taking a vacation lest you kill it. If you want to take a bread-baking hiatus, stick your starter in the fridge and forget about it. Really. It will be fine in there for months. Just take it out a day or two before you need it, feed it again, and that mother will be ready to "sourify" your dough.

So don't be intimidated by the recipes requiring the starter. They will taste especially amazing, and creating one is easier than you think.

Get Baking!

What are you waiting for? There are pitas, focaccias, brioches, marble ryes, and sweet potato biscuits in your future. Rebel against instant gratification and take the time to dig into doughs, watch them rise, and breathe in that incomparable bread-baking aroma. There is nothing like fresh bread, and this book has all the recipes and know-how to create 30 amazing carbs. So bake them. Before you die.

THE EASIEST WAY TO CREATE A SOURDOUGH STARTER (AND KEEP IT ALIVE!)

This is it. The beginning of everything. Or at the very least, the beginning of our sourdough bread journey. We have to start with the starter, and this is your seven-day guide to creating it.

But first! What the heck is a starter and why do we need it? There's a lot of science and microbes and fermentation that goes into it, but at the very basic level, the starter is a live culture of flour and water. It catches the wild yeast in the air and harvests it to make the bread rise, while also imparting a really nice bite to its flavor. We need it to make our best bread, and so we're going to spend five or so minutes each day for a week to create it.

Day 1: Grab a jar (a wide mouth works best for pouring and mixing), a kitchen scale, and whole wheat flour. (You can also use a 50/50 blend of whole wheat and all-purpose flours, a 50/50 blend of rye and all-purpose flours, or bread flour.) Measure 70 grams of the flour and 70 grams of warm water, and combine them in your jar. Mix it up into a thick paste, stick the lid or some plastic wrap loosely

on, and set it in a warm spot (shoot for 75°F to 80°F) for a day. A popular storage spot is in a turned-off oven with the light on.

Day 2: Observe the starter. Are there bubbles? Bubbles are good! They mean the fermentation has started. But it's okay if they're not quite there yet. Is there a weird-looking, dark liquid? Bread people call that "hooch," and it's just a sign that you need to feed your starter, which you'll do tomorrow. But today you're just watching.

Day 3: Now we're going to feed our starter! The first thing to do is throw away roughly half of what we've got. This is called "discard" in the bread world, and while some use it for other baked goods, you can also just throw it away. Discarding the old starter not only makes room for more flour and water, which the bacteria need in fresh rounds to feed upon, but it also decreases the acidity, which could hurt our microbes.

Now we have room to add another 70 grams of flour (you can use all-purpose, bread, or whole wheat) and another 70 grams of warm water. You don't need to be too fussy about the amount, either. You could use 30, 40, 50, or 60 grams; just make sure to use even quantities of flour and water. Mix it all up, cover it, and set it aside again.

Days 4 to 6: We should be seeing bubbles on and off during this period, but don't fret if some days are better than others. Just stick to the plan. Now we can feed our starter twice a day, at 12-hour intervals, with that same 1:1 ratio of flour and water (just remember to discard half before you feed). Repeat this same process for at least three days.

Day 7: Our little starter should be bubbling over with joy now! You'll know it's ready if it's doubled in size, has lots of bubbles, and is nice and fluffy. If you feel like it needs more time, keep feeding it for another day or two. Once ready, name it (mine is named Smeagol, after my pug), add it to your favorite recipe, and then bake and eat your little Smeagol.

Maintenance: If you're going to be using your starter regularly, keep it at room temperature and feed it the same way you did on days three to six, once or twice each day. If you're not going to need it for a while, just stick it in the fridge. (Smeagol is hardy and can survive for months there.) Then, a couple days before you need it again, repeat the feeding process to bring it back to life.

CHAPTER 1

Loaves

Beginner's Sourdough

Maurizio Leo, cookbook author and baking blogger (*The Perfect Loaf*)

Makes 2 loaves

Active time: 90 minutes
Total time: 1 day, 2 hours,
and 30 minutes

For the levain:

38 grams stone-ground
whole wheat flour

38 grams bread flour

76 grams water (For a 70°F
home, 94°F water; for every 2
degrees cooler, add 4 degrees
to the water temperature, and
for every 2 degrees warmer,
subtract 4 degrees from
the water temperature)

38 grams ripe sourdough starter

For the dough:

773 grams bread flour

114 grams whole wheat flour

51 grams whole grain rye flour

653 grams water (same water
temperature as above)

18 grams fine sea salt

Special equipment:

cooking thermometer

bulk fermentation container

bench scraper/knife

2 proofing baskets

Dutch oven or cast-
iron combo cooker

Don't be intimidated by sourdough. Let me say it again: DON'T BE INTIMIDATED BY SOURDOUGH. Yes, the recipe takes up a few pages. Yes, it takes a while. But the concepts required are kind of...simple. Yes, sourdough bread can be simple. It just takes a little pluck and patience.

First, what is sourdough bread? Obviously, it's delicious, with a bit of a tang from the wild yeast (i.e., you're not using store-bought yeast in this recipe) developed from natural fermentation. This natural fermentation comes from your starter (see page 11 for how to get this going), which is just a mixture of flour and water that develops wild yeast and good bacteria over time. This also helps with that chewy texture.

This recipe from the sourdough perfectionist Maurizio Leo lays out all the steps you need to make your first loaf in a handy timeline format. Of course, you don't need to start at 8 a.m., and you're free to adjust accordingly, but it's nice to know exactly when your bread is going to need your attention.

Once you have your starter, Leo begins with the levain (or leaven), which is a mixture of a small amount of your starter with water and flour. I think of it as a pre-dough. It will all end up in your dough and get baked into your bread. Temperature is a key component to making good sourdough, so you'll need an instant-read kitchen thermometer. Your goal: To get your dough to 74°F to 76°F, and then to around 78°F during the autolyze step.

The autolyze step sounds confusing but it's actually as simple as can be—you do absolutely nothing while the dough rests, creating some enzyme action to draw out sugars from the flour. This almost do-nothing step is awesome.

Next, you mix your dough with your levain, salt, and water. Take its temperature to see if it's around that 78°F mark and then set it in your bulk fermentation container. Again, totally easy!

During the bulk fermentation step, bacteria and yeast do their thing, which gives the bread its ability to rise and its awesome flavor. There's a lot of resting involved in this step, as well as some folding and stretching of the dough.

Now your dough is probably pretty sticky, so get your hands wet before touching it. That will help prevent the dough from sticking to them. At 30-minute increments as outlined in the recipe, you'll gently stretch a side of the dough and then fold it over onto itself.

You'll do this four times during each stretch-and-fold, rotating the dough 90 degrees with each turn. Just lift, fold, turn; lift, fold, turn, until you've gone 360 degrees.

There's a whole lot more resting (proofing/fermentation), shaping (a round loaf, or a boule, is a good starter loaf shape), scoring, and then baking. This all may seem complicated, but so did programming the microwave clock during daylight savings, and now just look at you with the correct time. Really the hardest part is waiting and timing the steps out, but it's all worth it when you can wow your friends, family, and frenemies with bakery-quality sourdough. (Or keep it all for yourself; you earned that bread!)

One of the best parts of mastering this loaf is all the customizing you can do with it. You can throw in some olives, jalapeño, and cheddar, or a swirl of rye (see recipe on page 27). For extra tips on any step of the bread-making process, Maurizio's website, www.ThePerfectLoaf.com, has excellent tutorials.

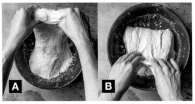

Levain (8:00 a.m.)

1. In a small container, mix the levain ingredients and keep at 74°F to 76°F (23°C to 24°C) for five to six hours.

Autolyze (12:00 p.m.)

2. In a large mixing bowl, mix the flours and 603 grams of water (reserve 50 grams until the next step). You want the dough to be at 78°F, but don't stress too much if it strays a couple degrees. Cover and let rest for one hour.

Mix (1:00 p.m.)

3. To the mixing bowl holding your dough, add the salt and ripe levain (from step 1). Slowly mix in the 50 grams of reserved water (if the dough is wet, you don't need to put in the full 50). Mix by hand or with a dough whisk until incorporated. Transfer your dough to a bulk fermentation container and cover.

Bulk Fermentation (1:10 p.m. to 5:10 p.m.)

4. Give the dough three sets of stretch and folds at 30-minute intervals, where the first set starts 30 minutes after the start of bulk fermentation. (See

paragraph eight in the headnotes and Sourdough process A and B photos.)

Divide and Preshape (5:10 p.m.)

5. Check the dough for some bubbles on the top and for a 20% to 50% increase in size. If it doesn't have those signs, leave it for another 15 minutes and then check again. Once it's ready, lightly flour your work surface and scrape out your dough. Using your bench knife, divide the dough in half. Then lightly shape each half into a round shape by tucking the edges under. Let the dough rest for 25 minutes, uncovered.

Shape (5:35 p.m.)

6. Shape the dough into a round (boule). To do this, take the left side of the dough and gently stretch it outward and then fold it toward the center. Do the same thing with the right side, so you have something like a swaddle going. Next take the bottom of your dough, gently stretch, and fold it onto the middle. Finally, take the top of the dough, stretch, and fold onto the center. (See photos 1 to 5.) Place seam side up in proofing baskets lined with clean kitchen towels and dusted lightly with flour.

Rest and Proof* (5:40 p.m. to 9:30 a.m. the next day)

7. Cover proofing baskets with reusable plastic and seal shut. Let the dough sit out on the counter for 20 minutes. Then, place both baskets into the refrigerator and proof overnight.

Bake (Preheat oven at 8:30 a.m., bake at 9:30 a.m.)

8. Place a combo cooker or Dutch oven on the bottom third rack of your oven and preheat to 450°F (232°C). When the oven is preheated, remove one of your proofing baskets from the fridge and place a piece of parchment paper over it. With an inverted baking sheet on top of the parchment, gently flip it over so your dough is resting on the parchment paper.

Using a razor or sharp knife, score the dough by slashing four lines in a large tic-tac-toe shape into the top. Transfer your dough to the preheated combo cooker. Place the cooker in the oven, cover with the lid, and bake for 20 minutes. After this time, remove the lid (you can keep it in the oven or remove it) and continue to bake for 30 minutes longer. When done, the internal temperature should be around 208°F (97°C). Repeat with the second loaf. Let the loaves cool for one to two hours on a wire rack before slicing.

*Note: While the recipe calls for 16 hours of total proof time, you could extend this time and bake the loaves in the morning, afternoon, or even the evening on day two. Leave the proofing dough in the fridge until ready to bake.

Smoked Oat Sourdough

Joshua Bellamy, Boulted Bread in Raleigh, NC

Makes 1 large loaf

Active time: 90 minutes
Total time: 2 days, 35 minutes

300 grams porridge, made from 150 grams whole or cracked oat groats (rolled oats work in a pinch but don't provide the same bite)

600 grams high-extraction flour (Look for 80% to 85% extraction; if you can't find that, a 50/50 blend of bread flour and whole wheat flour will work)

510 grams water, 90°F

72 grams starter (see page 11)

14 grams salt

handful rolled oats

Special equipment:

cooking thermometer

electric, wood, or charcoal smoker

bench scraper/knife

cheesecloth

Dutch oven or cast-iron combo cooker

Of course, you already know that bread isn't just *bread*. Bread is both life and alive, a carb that satisfies unlike any other, full of textures and flavors that transcend its base ingredients. But this smoked oat sourdough from Boulted Bread goes beyond even that. This is a hearty, hefty bread, one with all the smack you expect from a sourdough, but with the smoky weight of porridge mixed into the dough.

Yes, you are essentially mixing oatmeal into this dough, and the result is a bread that makes a lovely accompaniment, snack, or sidekick, sure, but also a meal in itself. It's the bread you want to rip into in the dead of winter or toast up for breakfast in summer. It's the bread you'll dream of if you ever find yourself, God forbid, stranded on a desert island without a smoker or high extraction flour. It's worth digging up the best quality ingredients you can find, but there are also some easy swaps for when you need to make a loaf *right now*. (Or as right now as a bread that takes more than two days to make can get.)

24 Hours Before Mixing

1. Cook 150 grams of whole or cracked oat groats in 450 grams of water, just like you're making oatmeal. Bring the water to a boil, add the groats, boil until the groats begin to swell, then reduce heat to medium and cook until a thick/porridge consistency is reached.

2. Transfer the porridge to a small sheet tray and smoke the porridge for 2 to 4 hours in a smoker (electric, wood, or charcoal), at a temperature of around 225°F. During the smoking process, the surface of the porridge will dry off and darken a bit; this is fine.

3. After 2 to 4 hours in the smoker, move the smoked oak porridge to an airtight container and store overnight at room temperature.

6 to 12 Hours Before Mixing

4. Refresh your sourdough starter. You want it at peak ripeness when you mix the dough.

Mixing

5. Combine the flour, 500 grams of water, and starter in a mixing bowl and hand mix until all of the flour is hydrated and there are no large clumps. The dough should look like a shaggy mess. Allow to rest for 20 minutes.

6. Add the salt and another 10 grams of water and hand mix until the salt and water are evenly distributed throughout the dough.

7. Fold the sides of the dough up onto itself for about 5 minutes, wetting your hands as necessary.

8. Scrape down the sides of the mixing bowl and cover with plastic wrap or a towel. Let rest for 20 minutes.

9. Incorporate 300 grams of the smoked oat porridge by gently squeezing it into the dough with a wet hand. Fold the sides of the dough in on itself 10 times to make sure the porridge is evenly distributed.

Bulk Fermentation

10. Place your covered dough in a 75°F to 80°F spot in your kitchen or house. At 30, 60, 120, and 180 minutes, wet your hands and fold the sides of the dough in on itself, 4 to 5 folds per time. Keep the mixing bowl covered between folds.

Dividing and Preshaping

11. After about 3 to 3.5 hours, the dough should be smooth and gassy. You can either make a large 3-pound loaf, or you can divide the dough in half with a knife or bench scraper for two smaller loaves.

12. Generously flour your shaping surface and dump the dough onto it. Using floured hands, gently fold the four sides of the dough into the center to create something that roughly resembles a square. Let rest, uncovered, for 20 minutes.

Shape

13. Line a proofing basket or large bowl with cheesecloth or a kitchen towel. Dust the surface with a layer of flour and rolled oats.

14. Shape the dough by gently folding the four corners into the center of the dough (or into your preferred shape). Gently pick up the dough and place in the proofing basket with the seam facing up.

Proof

15. Leave the loaf out at room temperature for 60 minutes. After that hour, cover and refrigerate the loaf for 12 to 24 hours.

Bake

16. Preheat oven to 500°F.

17. Using a covered Dutch oven, bake the loaf for 30 to 35 minutes, or until it achieves your desired level of browning. Let it fully cool before slicing...or just rip into it while it's warm and smear with butter!

Marble Rye Sourdough

Zach Martinucci, Rebel Bread in Denver, CO

Makes 2 loaves

Active time: 95 minutes
Total time: 1 day, 2 hours,
40 minutes

Note: This recipe uses Maurizio Leo's Beginner Sourdough Bread recipe on page 17 as a base

52 grams rye flour

8 grams caraway seeds

20 grams cocoa powder

24 grams diastatic malt powder

4 grams salt

120 grams water

A pure loaf of sourdough is a beautiful thing, but so is gussying up that sourdough to your liking. Here, we're swirling rye flour, caraway seeds, and cocoa powder into the dough via our folds, creating a visually stunning slice once it's baked and cooled. (Or not cooled; it's totally fine if self-control and patience are not your virtues.)

While Zach uses his own base sourdough recipe at his Denver bakery, you've already mastered Maurizio Leo's fantastic beginner's sourdough bread (or if you haven't, now's the time!), so we're going to use that as our base and add Zach's rye batter. The rye addition comes at the end of step two, and all you'll do is add your batter to the top of the dough. It gets mixed in via the stretches and folds, which is what creates those marbled serpentine swirls.

1. Follow steps 1 (levain) and 2 (autolyze) in the beginner sourdough recipe on page 17.

2. After step 2, once your dough has rested for 1 hour, you will prepare the marble rye inclusion. In a separate bowl, mix together the rye flour, caraway seeds, cocoa powder, diastatic malt powder, salt, and water until homogenous and well-hydrated. It will be more of a batter than a dough. Set aside.

3. Follow step 3 (mix) in the beginner sourdough recipe. Before covering your dough in the bulk fermentation container, add the marble rye inclusion in a single layer on top of the base dough. Do not mix. The inclusion will get folded into the dough in layers by the folds during bulk fermentation, creating a marbling effect throughout the dough. Cover the container.

4. Follow the rest of the steps in the beginner sourdough recipe, noting that the rye loaf may take an additional 5 to 10 minutes to cook.

Baguette

Shawn Bergin, Bakery Four in Denver, CO

Makes 4 demi-baguettes

Active time: 1 hour
Total time: 2 days, 3 hours

For the autolyze (100% bakers percentage):

500 grams flour of your choice, preferably a soft wheat mixed with a bread flour (you can also add a bit of rye, spelt, or kamut flour)

250 grams water, 120°F to 130°F

For the poolish (33% bakers percentage at 100% hydration):

82.5 grams flour, same blend as used for the autolyze

82.5 grams warm water, 90°F to 110°F

1 gram yeast (either instant or active dry will work)

For the natural levain (21% bakers percentage at 100% hydration):

45 grams bread flour

45 grams hot water, 120°F to 130°F

15 grams ripe sourdough starter (see page 11)

For the final mix:

1.5 grams dry yeast

17 grams ice cold water

15 grams sea salt

Special equipment:

stand mixer

pizza stone

Many bakers consider the baguette to be the most difficult bread to make. Besides impeccable shaping, scoring, and baking, you want that crispy bronzed crust to burst when bit into, yielding soft, custardy innards. It's a lot to expect from flour, salt, and water, but here's the thing. Even your wonky-shaped, initial baguettes are going to be very good baguettes. Throw perfection aside for a moment, surrender to the process, and baguettes don't seem so hard.

Shawn breaks it into a 3-day operation, with pretty simple (and quick!) instructions for what to do each day. You can view the recipe as three separate components within one dough: the autolyze, the poolish, and the levain. All are variations on the very simple formula of combining water and flour, and once you have all three, you mix them together to create the final dough.

There are several fermentation and mixing techniques in this formula to help you get that crackly crust and soft interior texture while maximizing the creamy flavor of good wheat. Most of them involve you doing nothing, and time, the air, and a stand mixer taking on the heavy lifting. But you get to choose the flours (you can experiment with different types and ratios; I used 80% bread flour and 20% whole wheat) and do a couple of those stretch and folds that you might have already practiced in one of the earlier sourdough recipes.

You also do the shaping, which comes on day 3 in step 7. You'll flatten each piece of dough (this recipe makes 4 demi-baguettes) into a rectangle, and then fold, seal, and roll the baguette to thin it out, from the center of the log out.

My first attempt was not gorgeous, and yours may not be either. But there's something about the process that just might hook you, prompting you to start the 3-day process again and again until you do get that impeccable baguette. You just have to start with that wonky one.

Day 1

1. Autolyze: Pour the 500 grams of flour and 250 grams of water into the bowl of a stand mixer. Using the bread hook attachment, mix on high until fully incorporated. Feel free to let this go for 10 minutes or so; the dough should feel somewhat stiff and slightly tacky to the touch. Place the dough in an oiled bowl, cover, and refrigerate overnight.

2. Overnight poolish: Mix 82.5 grams of flour, 82.5 grams of warm water, and 1 gram of yeast in a bowl until it's the consistency of muffin batter. Let sit for 15 to 20 minutes at room temperature. Place in a storage container that will allow for the poolish to double in size (at least), and refrigerate overnight.

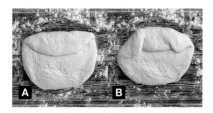

Day 2

3. Natural Levain: In a clear container or bowl, mix 45 grams flour, 45 grams hot water, and 15 grams of your starter until it's the consistency of muffin batter. Place in a turned-off oven with the light on for 2 to 2.5 hours. Remove from the oven once you see some bubbles developing. (Utilize the float test if you're unsure of activity—place a small amount of levain in a cup of room temperature water; it will float when ready.)

4. Final Mix: Once your levain is ready, remove the autolyze from your oiled bowl and place in the bowl of a stand mixer. Add your overnight poolish and levain to the autolyze. Mix on low until all ingredients are incorporated and smooth, then let rest 30 minutes. After the rest, start the mixer at medium speed and add 1.5 grams of yeast. Slowly add the 17 grams of cold water, then mix for 4 to 6 minutes. Add 15 grams of salt and mix 2 to 3 minutes more, until the salt is evenly distributed.

5. Place the dough in a large, oiled container and cover. The dough should be cold to the touch and somewhat slack. Place in the refrigerator for 30 minutes to rest, then remove and turn the dough out onto a lightly floured surface. To fold, take the left side of the dough and gently stretch it outward, then fold into the center. Do the same thing on the right side, top, and bottom. Put the dough back in the oiled container, cover, and refrigerate overnight.

Day 3

6. Turn out the dough onto a clean surface and cut into 4 pieces. (Weigh the first piece; you're shooting for 200 to 250 grams per cut.) Roll each piece of dough into a ball and let rest for 20 to 30 minutes before final shaping. Preheat oven, with a pizza stone inside, to 500°F.

7. After resting, the dough should be relaxed enough to shape. Flour your surface and flatten the dough out into a rectangle. Roll the top of the dough about one-third of the way down with the pinky side of your hands to build tension. (See photo Baguette process A) Gently stretch and pull each of the top corners down onto that fold. (See photo Baguette process B) Roll the dough again in the same way so that it's nearly in a log shape. Seal the edge with your palm and roll, from the center of the dough outward, into a pointed log, about 12 inches long. (See photo Baguette process C) Use rice (or any) flour to coat a kitchen towel, and place the baguettes on the towel seam side up. Let proof until the dough springs back when poked lightly, about 1½ to 2 hours.

8. Turn the dough onto your preheated pizza stone and score to your preference with scissors, a sharp knife, or a razor blade. Place a cake pan filled with water in the oven to create steam while baking. Bake for 30 minutes, the first 20 with the steam, and then remove the pan for the remaining 10 minutes. Take out your baguettes and enjoy.

Focaccia

Joanne Chang, Flour Bakery in Boston, MA, from *Flour, Too,* published by Chronicle Books

Makes 1 large sandwich loaf

Active time: 20 minutes
Total time: 4 hours

1 teaspoon active dry yeast

1½ cups (360 milliliters) tepid water

3 cups (420 grams) all-purpose flour

1 cup (150 grams) bread flour

5 teaspoons granulated sugar

2 teaspoons kosher salt

½ cup (120 milliliters) olive oil

small handful cornmeal, for sprinkling on the baking sheet

You could say that focaccia bread has been having a moment. Social media is full of puffy, bubble-rific doughs looking like gassy wet clouds about to burst. Joanne Chang's focaccia is not made for social media, though; it is made for sandwiches. It will not bubble up like chewed Trident but instead will be perfectly dimply, chewy, and salty, especially when housing smoked turkey, chicken, avocado, and/or cheddar cheese. Or, just rip off a chunk and dip it into more olive oil and call it a sandwich. That works, too.

1. In the bowl of the stand mixer, combine 1½ cups (360 ml) tepid water and yeast and let sit for 20 to 30 seconds to allow yeast to dissolve and activate. Dump all-purpose flour, bread flour, sugar, and salt into water. Carefully turn the mixer on to low speed and mix for about 10 seconds. (To prevent flour from flying out of the bowl, turn the mixer on and off several times until flour is mixed into liquid, and then keep it on low speed.) When dough is still shaggy looking, drizzle in olive oil, aiming it along the side of the bowl to keep it from splashing and making a mess.

2. With the mixer still on low speed, knead dough for 4 to 5 minutes, or until it is smooth and supple. The dough should be somewhat sticky but still smooth and have an elastic, stretchy texture. (If it is much stiffer than this, mix 1 to 2 tablespoons water; if it is much looser than this, mix in 2 to 3 tablespoons all-purpose flour.)

3. Lightly oil a large bowl. Transfer dough to the oiled bowl, cover with an oiled piece of plastic wrap or a damp lint-free cloth, and place in a draft-free, warm (78° to 82°F is ideal) area for 2 to 3 hours. An area near the stove or in the oven with only the oven light on is good. The dough should rise until it is about double in bulk. (This is called proofing the dough.)

4. Once dough has risen, flour your hands and the work surface and turn the dough out onto the work surface. Press dough into an 8-inch square and fold the top edge of the square down to the center of the dough. Fold the bottom of the square up to the center of dough and press the seam firmly with your fingers. Now fold the right side of the square into the center and the left side into the center, and again press the seam firmly. Turn dough over, seam-side down, and shape dough with a tucking motion so that it is about 6 inches square. Sprinkle a baking sheet with cornmeal and transfer dough to it. Generously flour the top of the dough, and then cover dough loosely but completely with a damp lint-free cloth or a piece of plastic wrap. Place in a warm area for another hour or so, or until dough rises a bit and gets puffy and pillowy. (This is proofing, again.)

5. Preheat oven to 400°F and place a rack in the center of the oven. When dough is ready, remove the cloth or plastic wrap. Using all ten fingers, press and poke and elongate the dough three or four times along its length so that you press and stretch it into an almost-square log that is about 10 inches long, 8 inches wide, and about 2 inches tall. Bake for 35 to 45 minutes, or until completely golden brown on the top and bottom. Lift the loaf and make sure the underside is browned before pulling it out of the oven, or you will end up with a soggy loaf. Let cool on the pan on a wire rack for about 30 minutes, or until cool enough to handle, then cut into slices ¾-inch thick for sandwiches. The focaccia loaf will keep in a closed paper bag at room temperature for up to 3 days, or tightly wrapped in two layers of plastic wrap in the freezer for up to 2 weeks.

From *Flour, Too* © 2013 by Joanne Chang and Michael Harlan Turkell. Used with permission of Chronicle Books LLC, San Francisco. Visit ChronicleBooks.com

3-Ingredient Bread

Kimberlee Ho, baking blogger (*Kickass Baker*)

Makes 1 loaf

Active time: 10 minutes
Total time: 1 hour

5 tablespoons melted unsalted butter, divided (optional)

3 cups self-rising flour

3 tablespoons sugar

1 (12-ounce) mild lager (1½ cups), such as Budweiser

Special equipment:

nonstick loaf pan

Three ingredients, no rising time, and no kneading. Beer bread is the low-maintenance, woke-up-like-this of breads. Although it's better with a fourth ingredient—butter—it shouldn't really count because, come on, everything is better with butter. The yeast in the beer, plus the self-rising flour and sugar, make the bread magically rise without additional yeast, and the taste is incredible. Hearty and slightly sweet, with just a tinge of lager, only carbier.

1. Adjust oven rack to middle position and preheat to 400°F. Brush melted butter liberally on the bottom and sides of an 8½ x 4½ -inch nonstick loaf pan. Set loaf pan and remaining melted butter aside.

2. Stir flour and sugar together in a large bowl. Stir in beer and mix until a shaggy, sticky dough forms. Cover with plastic wrap and allow to sit for 15 minutes.

3. Transfer dough to the prepared loaf pan. Brush 3 tablespoons melted butter over the top, smoothing the bread dough a bit as you brush on the melted butter. Reserve about 1 tablespoon of the melted butter for brushing on the finished loaf.

4. Bake until a toothpick inserted in the center of the loaf comes out with no crumbs attached and the top is light golden brown, 35 to 40 minutes. After removing from the oven, immediately brush the top of the loaf with remaining melted butter.

5. Transfer pan to wire rack and let cool for 5 minutes. Turn loaf out onto a wire rack, turn right side up, and let cool completely on rack, at least 1 hour. Slice and serve.

Hokkaido Milk Bread

Sarah Kozuma, Horseshoe Cafe in Newmarket, NH

Makes 1 loaf

Active time: 1 hour
Total time: 5 hours

For the tangzhong:

30 grams bread flour

70 grams whole milk

70 grams water

For the dough:

435 grams bread flour

60 grams sugar

1 tablespoon instant yeast

5 grams kosher salt

1 large egg

140 grams whole milk

36 grams (about 2½ tablespoons) unsalted butter, softened

Special equipment:

2-pound Pullman loaf pan

For the softest, the wispiest, the squishiest, the most magical loaf of white bread in existence, it's this Hokkaido milk bread. Named for the region in Japan prized for its rich, creamy milk, this ultra-fluffy loaf is sweet and delicious. You can use it for a sandwich or as a base for toast, or just tear chunks of it off by the fistful.

One of the keys is the tangzhong, which is sort of like a roux that you cook up before adding it to your dough. This will make your bread softer (i.e., this is not a crusty loaf), and it'll help it stay fresh longer, too. For that nice square shape, bake it up in a Pullman loaf pan, but really whatever loaf pan you have on hand will work.

1. Make the tangzhong by whisking the bread flour, milk, and water in a small saucepan. Set the pan over low heat, whisking constantly until it thickens, 4 to 6 minutes. Allow to cool.

2. In the bowl of a stand mixer, add bread flour, sugar, yeast, salt, egg, whole milk, and cooled tangzhong. Knead on low speed with the bread hook attachment for 5 minutes. Cover the dough with a dish towel or plastic wrap and allow to rest for 10 minutes.

3. Add the softened butter and knead on low for about 20 minutes. The dough should be stretchy, smooth, pliable, and just slightly tacky.

4. Shape into a ball, place in a lightly greased container, and cover. Allow to rise at room temperature until the dough is doubled in size, maybe even tripled! The time will vary based on your kitchen temperature, but probably 1 to 3 hours.

5. Once the dough has risen, punch it down and divide it into four equal portions (probably around 210 grams

or so). Shape each into a ball, cover, and let rest for about 15 minutes.

6. On a lightly floured surface, flatten each ball into a long oval, about 6 x 9 inches or so. Fold the long sides in so it looks something like a swaddle, pinch them together, and roll lightly with a rolling pin to flatten it a bit again. Roll up into a log shape about 4.5 inches long, or to fit your loaf pan. Repeat for every log. Place the logs in a lightly greased 2-pound Pullman loaf pan. Cover and allow to rise until the dough is just peeking over the top of the pan, about 1 to 2 hours.

7. Preheat oven to 325°F for convection or 350°F for a regular oven. (If using a regular oven, fill a pan with water and place in the oven for the first 5 minutes of baking for some steam.) Lightly brush the top with milk and bake for 30 to 35 minutes, until the internal temperature reaches 207°F. Cool in pan for at least 10 minutes before removing.

Soft Sandwich Bread, Gluten-Free

Jeanne Sauvage, cookbook author and baking blogger (*Art of Gluten-Free Baking*)

Makes 1 loaf

Active time: 20 minutes
Total time: 1 hour, 50 minutes

¾ **cup (110 grams)**
brown rice flour

¾ **cup (125 grams) white rice flour**

¾ **cup (115 grams) sweet white**
rice flour (aka glutinous rice flour)

¾ **cup (90 grams) tapioca**
flour (aka tapioca starch),
plus more for dusting

2 teaspoons xanthan gum (this
serves as a gluten-replacer)

3 tablespoons granulated sugar

2 tablespoons instant yeast
(be sure it is gluten-free)

1 tablespoon aluminum-free
double-acting baking powder

1 teaspoon fine sea salt

2 large eggs

1½ cups (360 milliliters) warm
but not hot water (about 95°F)

¼ **cup (60 milliliters) olive**
or other neutral oil, plus
more for brushing

1 teaspoon apple cider vinegar

Special equipment:

stand mixer

When Jeanne Sauvage was diagnosed as gluten-intolerant more than 20 years ago, what she missed most was good bread. Even something as seemingly simple as making a sandwich became tricky, and she couldn't find a grocery store bread that she actually wanted to eat. So she set out to create her own gluten-free sandwich bread that tasted delicious but was also easy to make. (This bread takes less than 2 hours to mix, rise, and bake.) Now a staple of her kitchen, this sandwich bread could become a staple of yours—even if you don't have to eat gluten-free.

1. Brush an 8 x 4 x 4-inch (or roughly those measurements) metal loaf pan with oil and then lightly dust with tapioca flour. If your pan has vent holes in the bottom, brush the inside of the pan with oil, place a piece of parchment paper sized to fit the bottom of the pan, brush the parchment paper with a bit more oil, and then dust the inside with tapioca flour.

2. In a medium bowl, whisk together flours, xanthan gum, granulated sugar, instant yeast, baking powder, and salt.

3. In the bowl of a stand mixer fitted with the paddle attachment, place the eggs, water, oil, and vinegar. Use a fork to lightly pre-mix the wet ingredients. Add dry ingredients to the wet ingredients. Start the mixer on the lowest setting to begin the mixing process (so the ingredients don't hop out of the bowl), and then raise speed to high to beat the dough for 4 minutes. After mixing, the dough will look like smooth (albeit sticky) buttercream frosting.

4. Preheat oven to 375°F. Scrape the dough into the prepared pan and gently smooth the top. Lightly brush the top of the dough with oil and loosely cover the pan with plastic wrap. Place the pan in a warm, draft-free place to rise for about 30 to 40 minutes, or until the dough has almost doubled in size. Do not let the dough rise above the top of the pan because it needs the pan walls to hold its structure.

5. Remove plastic wrap and bake bread for about 50 minutes, or until an instant-read thermometer reads at least 200°F when inserted into the middle of the bread. Check the bread about 25 minutes into the baking process, and if the top of the bread looks like it is getting too brown, place a piece of tented aluminum foil over the top.

6. Carefully turn out bread onto a wire rack and cool completely before cutting. If possible, cool for several hours. If you cut the bread before it is completely cool, it will be a bit sticky inside. This stickiness will dissipate over time. Bread is best stored at room temperature, cut-side down on a cutting board or in a paper bag. To store the bread longer than about 3 days, cut the loaf into slices, place slices into a zip-top bag, and freeze.

Honey Whole Wheat Loaf

Anne Ng and Jeremy Mandrell, Bakery Lorraine in Austin, TX

Makes 2 (13 x 4-inch) loaves

Active time: 25 minutes
Total time: 3 hours, 20 minutes

1,077 grams all-purpose flour

392 grams whole wheat flour

59 grams sugar

26 grams kosher salt

24 grams instant yeast

940 grams water

57 grams honey

118 grams unsalted butter, softened and cubed

Special equipment:

stand mixer

Pullman loaf pan

The building block of every good sandwich is, of course, good bread. If you start with this wheat loaf from Austin's Bakery Lorraine, it doesn't really matter what you slap between the slices, it's going to be great because of the bread. Sad turkey that's pushing its expiration date? Still delish! Kraft singles? Never tasted better. While this recipe, which makes two large loaves, will push the capabilities of a standard electric mixer, it can be done. (And it's worth a little flour sloshing.)

1. Mix both flours, sugar, salt, and yeast in a mixing bowl. Into the bowl of a stand mixer, combine water and honey.

2. Add the flour mixture into the wet ingredients and start mixing on low speed with the dough hook. Add the butter a few cubes at a time. Mix on low until a smooth ball of dough forms. It should slap away from the sides of the bowl and look shiny and smooth.

3. Weigh out 1,300 grams of dough per Pullman loaf. Immediately shape into loaves by gently pressing the dough into a flat disc. Pull out the right bottom side of the dough and fold into the middle; repeat on the left side. You should have a sort of rectangular shape, about the length of your pan. Roll the dough top-down, tucking the dough into itself every time you roll. (You should feel tension in the dough with every roll and tuck.) It should end up resembling a cylinder. Pinch at the seams to close it all up and drop into oiled Pullman loaf pans, seam side down.

4. Proof at room temperature, covered with a damp towel, until it doubles in volume, about 1½ to 2 hours.

5. Bake at 400°F for about 50 minutes. (Leave the lid off to allow for maximum volume when baked.) Immediately unmold from pans and let cool before slicing.

Brioche with Honey Butter

Kelli Marks, Sweet Love Bakes in Little Rock, AR

Makes 1 (10 x 4-inch) loaf

Active time: 15 minutes
Total time: 3 hours, 50 minutes

1 cup milk, warm

2¼ teaspoons active dry yeast

2 tablespoons honey

1 egg

2¾ cups (420 grams) all-purpose flour, plus more for dusting

2 teaspoons salt

4 tablespoons softened unsalted butter, divided

For the topping:

2 tablespoons butter

2 tablespoons honey

1 teaspoon maldon salt

Special equipment:

stand mixer

Brioche is like the lax, fun aunt of bread loaves. Feeling like indulging in an unholy amount of honey butter? Go for it! Craving something slightly savory with herbs and garlic? Throw them on in there! Want to add raisins? If you must, but to each their own. Really, you can add whatever you'd like to the center or the topping of this buttery bread, but for this recipe, Kelli Marks spreads on salted honey butter, which is about as good of a match for this soft, rich loaf as I can imagine. Your freewheeling aunt would approve.

1. In the bowl of a stand mixer fitted with a dough hook, place warm milk, yeast, and honey. Milk should be warm to the touch (I use the baby bottle method and test it on my wrist; it should be warm but not hot); if you're using a thermometer, aim for 105 °F to 115°F. Allow the yeast to bloom, meaning it will become bubbly and active, about 5 minutes.

2. Add the egg, flour, and salt. Allow the dough to come together and mix for about 3 minutes. Add 2 tablespoons of butter and allow to mix for another 2 to 3 minutes.

3. Transfer dough to a large bowl and cover tightly with plastic wrap. Place it in a warm area in your kitchen and allow to proof until dough is doubled in size, about 1 to 2 hours. (Or you can do a cold proof in the fridge, but that will take about 8 to 12 hours.)

4. Once dough has doubled, lightly dust your counter with flour and roll the dough into a rectangle roughly 10 by 16 inches. Spread the remaining 2 tablespoons of softened butter across the dough and roll up the long way, creating a dough log the length of your loaf pan. Place dough in pan.

5. In a small bowl, melt butter and honey and brush across the top of the loaf. Sprinkle with maldon salt. Keep leftover honey butter mixture to brush on top after baking.

6. Allow bread to proof uncovered a second time, again looking for the dough to double in size. This should take around 45 minutes. While this is proofing, heat the oven to 350°F.

7. Bake loaf for 30 to 35 minutes, or until the internal temperature is around 190°F. After bread cools slightly, brush top again with honey butter mixture.

Challah

Deb Perelman (Adapted from a recipe by Joan Nathan),
cookbook author and food blogger (*Smitten Kitchen*)

Makes 2 loaves

Active time: 30 minutes
Total time: 3 hours, 30 minutes

3¾ teaspoons active dry yeast
(about 1½ packages or 11 grams)

½ cup (100 grams) plus
1 tablespoon (13 grams)
granulated sugar, divided

1¾ cups lukewarm water

½ cup olive or vegetable oil, plus
more for greasing the bowl

4 large eggs

1 tablespoon (14 grams) table salt

8 to 8½ cups (1,000 to 1,063
grams) all-purpose flour

½ cup raisins (about 70 grams)
per challah, if using, plumped
in hot water and drained

To finish:

1 large egg

poppy or sesame seeds (optional)

Special equipment:

electric mixer

If you ever wondered what a braided cloud would taste like in bread form, well, that's challah for you. Eggy, fluffy, and slightly sweet, challah is everything you want out of an interwoven carb, and Deb Perelman (aka the woman behind the *Smitten Kitchen* blog) is our challah-back girlboss.

The dough itself is fairly easy to make—it just takes some patience and bread-braiding know-how. Some weaving tips: Once you've got your six dough strands lined up and the tops pinched together (step 4), grab the far right strand. Move it over the two strands to its left. Next, take the second strand from the left and move it all the way to the far right side, so it's now the farthest strand on the right. Take the outside left strand and move it over two. Then take the second strand from the right and move it all the way over to the far left. Start over with the outside right strand and repeat this process as many times as it takes to get to the bottom of that braid.

1. In a large bowl, dissolve yeast and 1 tablespoon sugar in water; set aside for 5 minutes until a bit foamy.

2. Whisk oil into yeast, then beat in 4 eggs, 1 at a time, with remaining half cup sugar and tablespoon of salt. Gradually add flour. When dough holds together, it is ready for kneading. (You can do this with an electric mixer fitted with the dough hook attachment.)

3. Turn dough onto a floured surface and knead until smooth. Clean out bowl and grease it, then return dough to bowl. Cover with plastic wrap, and let rise* in a warm place for 1 hour, until almost doubled in size. Dough may also rise in an oven that has been warmed to 150°F then turned off. Punch down dough, cover, and let rise again in a warm place for another half hour.

4. At this point, you can knead the raisins into the challah, if you're using them, before forming the loaves. To make a 6-braid challah, take half the dough and form it into 6 balls. With your hands, roll each ball into a strand about 12 inches long and 1½ inches wide. Place the 6 in a row, parallel to one another. Pinch the tops of the strands together. Move the outside right strand over two strands. Then take the second strand from the left and move it to the far right. Take the outside left strand and move it over two strands. Move second strand from the right over to the far left. Start over with the outside right strand. Continue this until all strands are braided. For a straight loaf, tuck ends underneath. (See process photos 1 to 4.) Make a second loaf the same way. Place braided loaves on a greased cookie sheet with at least 2 inches in between.

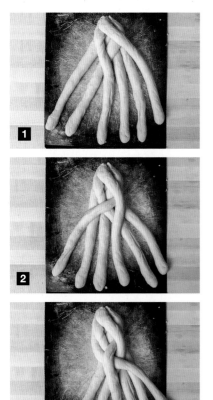

5. Beat remaining egg and brush it on the loaves. Either freeze the breads or let rise another hour.

6. If baking immediately, preheat oven to 375°F and brush loaves again with egg wash. Sprinkle bread with seeds, if using. If freezing, remove from freezer 5 hours before baking.

7. Bake on the middle oven rack for 30 to 40 minutes, or until golden. (If you have an instant-read thermometer, you can take it out when it hits an internal temperature of 190°F.) Cool loaves on a rack.

*Note: Any of the three risings can be done in the fridge for a few hours, for more deeply developed flavor. When you're ready to work with it again, bring the dough back to room temperature before moving onto the next step.

CHAPTER 2

Smaller Carbs

Ultimate Dinner Rolls

Tessa Arias, cookbook author and food blogger (*Handle the Heat*)

Makes 12 rolls

Active time: 30 minutes
Total time: 2 hours 50 minutes

¼ cup lukewarm water

1 cup warm milk (100°F to 110°F)

1 tablespoon unsalted butter, melted, plus more for greasing

2 large eggs, lightly beaten

2 tablespoons granulated sugar

1½ teaspoons fine salt

2¼ teaspoons (1 packet) instant yeast

4½ cups (572 grams) bread flour, divided

To finish:

1 egg, lightly beaten

melted butter

flaky sea salt

Special equipment:

stand mixer

bench scraper or pizza wheel

Everyone should have a dinner roll recipe on the culinary equivalent of speed dial, and this recipe bakes up deliciously fluffy rolls in five easy steps. Sweet, salty, and buttery, these little dough boys (or gals) are the perfect starch, side, or, heck, main course for your meal. Because no one puts these rolls in the corner.

1. Combine the water, milk, 1 tablespoon of the melted butter, eggs, sugar, salt, and yeast in the bowl of a stand mixer. Add 2 cups of the flour and stir with a wooden spoon until the dough forms a rough, shaggy mass.

2. Attach the dough hook to the mixer, turn to medium-low speed, and gradually add the remaining flour, kneading until a mass of dough begins to form. Continue kneading on medium-high speed for 4 to 5 minutes until a soft, smooth ball of dough is formed. The dough should feel elastic and slightly tacky to the touch.

3. Lightly spray a large clean bowl with cooking spray and place the dough in the bowl. Cover the bowl lightly with plastic wrap. Let rise for about 1 hour to 90 minutes at room temperature or until the dough is big, puffy, and about doubled in size.

4. Grease a 9 x 13-inch or similarly shaped baking pan with butter. Gently deflate the dough. Use a bench scraper, knife, or pizza wheel to divide the dough into 12 equal pieces. Shape each piece into a ball and place in the prepared pan. Lightly cover the dough with plastic wrap and let the rolls rise for about 1 hour, or until about doubled in size.

5. Preheat the oven to 375°F. Brush the rolls gently with the beaten egg. Bake the rolls for 20 minutes, or until golden brown. Brush with melted butter and sprinkle with salt. Serve warm.

Croissants

Dominique Ansel, Dominique Ansel Bakery in New York, NY, and Las Vegas, NV

Makes 15 croissants

Active time: 1 hour, 30 minutes
Total time: 1 day, 6 hours, 30 minutes

For the dough:

6½ cups bread flour

2½ teaspoons salt

⅓ cup sugar

¼ cup fresh yeast

5 teaspoons honey

⅓ cup butter, room temperature

⅗ cup water

¾ cup milk

1 large egg

For the butter block:

2 cups (4 sticks) butter, room temperature

For the egg wash:

1 large egg

1 teaspoon milk

¼ teaspoon salt

Special equipment:

stand mixer

dough scraper

You probably know Dominique Ansel as the creator of the Cronut®, the doughnut-croissant hybrid that ruled the internet in the 2010s. So I think you can trust the guy who put the "Cro" in Cronut® with your laminated pastries. After all, he perfected his croissant recipe long before the C-word ever even entered our collective vocabulary.

His croissants are everything that a croissant should be: flaky, golden, buttery, and a touch sweet. They do take time, a lot of rolling, practice, and patience (and a good amount of butter, too), but your finished crescents will warrant your now-stronger forearms and higher cholesterol levels.

1. To make the dough: In a stand mixer fitted with a dough hook, add in all your ingredients for the dough, putting in the dry ingredients first, then adding in the wet. Mix on slow speed until everything is incorporated, about 2 to 3 minutes. Then switch to mix on high speed until the dough is smooth with a little bit of elasticity, about 5 to 7 minutes.

2. Remove the dough from the mixer bowl and place on a flat working surface. Using your palms, tightly roll the dough into a ball so it becomes smooth and firm. If you press your finger deep into the dough, it should spring back. Once the dough is firm, use a knife to cut an "X" on top. Then spread open the edges so it forms a square. Place the dough on a half sheet tray lined with parchment paper. Lightly cover the top of the dough with plastic wrap.

3. For the first fermentation, leave the covered dough outside in a warm part of the room (e.g., near the oven) and let it proof until it has roughly doubled or almost tripled in size, about 2 hours.

Once it has proofed, press down the dough with your palms until it is flat and no longer has air. Straighten out the sides with your palms so it stays roughly the shape of a 7-inch square. Place the dough, still covered in plastic wrap pressed to the surface, in the refrigerator.

4. To make the butter block, place your room temperature butter in between 2 sheets of parchment paper. Using the palm of your hand, press down on the butter to flatten. Use a dough scraper to help straighten out the edges so that you form roughly a 7-inch square that is about 1/8-inch thick. Place your butter block in the refrigerator, still in between the 2 parchment pieces.

5. After about 1 hour in the refrigerator, the dough will go through a second fermentation and proof slightly (but not double in volume). Press it down once again. Let the dough and butter block rest in the refrigerator overnight so that it can relax and be easier to laminate the next day.

6. For lamination: Once the dough and butter block have rested overnight, remove both from the refrigerator. The dough should be as cold as possible (even if it needs a few minutes in the freezer). The butter block, on the other hand, may need to sit out for a few minutes so that it can slightly temper and bend without cracking. When the temperature of the dough and butter are right, you can begin to laminate. Lightly dust a flat surface with flour. Unwrap the dough and place it on the surface. You may want to lightly roll it out into the size of a 7-inch square if it has shrunk overnight. (As you roll, don't forget to slide the dough, adding more flour to the table as needed so it does not stick.) Arrange the butter block in the center of the dough so it looks like a diamond in the center of the square (rotated 45 degrees, with the corners of the butter block facing the center of the dough sides). Pull the corners of the dough up and over to the center of the butter block until you've wrapped up the butter block completely. Pinch the seams of the dough together to fully seal the butter inside. You should have a packet of dough and butter that is a slightly larger square at 7 to 8 inches.

7. With a rolling pin, using steady and even pressure, roll the croissant dough so that it quadruples in length. When finished you should have a rectangle that is roughly 28 inches long, 10 inches wide, and ¼ inch thick. Place the dough so the longer side runs left to right. Fold the right side in just a bit before the center of the dough, keeping the edges lined up. Fold the left side over to meet the right side. Then fold in half again. This is called a "double" or

"book" fold because it closes up like a book. Wrap the dough in plastic wrap and place it in the refrigerator for 25 to 30 minutes.

8. Remove the croissant dough from the refrigerator, unwrap, and place it on a lightly floured surface. Orient the dough so the seam is always on the right side (and the "opening" is on the top and bottom). Roll the dough out vertically again from the top to the bottom until it has tripled in length. When finished, you should have a rectangle that is roughly 21 inches long, 10 inches wide, and ¼ inch thick. Orient the dough so the longer side runs left to right. From the right side, fold 1/3 of the dough onto itself, keeping the edges lined up with each other. From the left side, fold the remaining 1/3 of the dough on top of the side already folded. Line up all the edges so you are left again with a square. This is called a "letter" or "single" fold because it is how you would fold a letter to place inside an envelope. Wrap the dough in plastic wrap and let it rest again in the refrigerator for 25 to 30 minutes.

9. Now it's time for the final sheeting. Remove the croissant dough from the refrigerator, unwrap, and place it on a lightly floured surface. Orient your dough so the seam is on the right and the "opening" is on the top and bottom. Roll out the croissant dough again lengthwise to roughly triple in length, or a rectangle that is 24 inches long, 10 inches wide, and ¼ inch thick.

10. Cutting a croissant: With the long end of the dough running left to right, it's now time to cut your croissant. Trim the top and bottom of the dough

so it is in a straight line. With a ruler, measure one side of an isosceles triangle that is roughly 10.5 inches and cut with a large knife. Next, measure out the base of the triangle, which should be 3 inches wide. Now cut the third side of the triangle. This will be the triangle for your regular croissant. To make it easier, you can make a mark every 3 inches and cut the remaining dough into isosceles triangles.

11. Place the cut dough pieces on top of a parchment-lined half sheet tray and put it back into the refrigerator to chill for 10 to 15 minutes, loosely covered in plastic wrap.

12. Get ready to roll your croissants! Remove the croissant triangles from the refrigerator. Holding onto the wider base with one hand, use the other hand's thumb and index finger to gently pull the dough to stretch and relax it. It should be 2 inches or so longer. Orient the base of the triangle toward you and slowly roll up from the base to the tip gently without being too tight.

13. Line a half sheet tray with parchment paper. It's time to "tray up" the croissant and prepare it for proof and bake. Place the croissant with its "tail" at the bottom of the tray so it does not unravel, and space each croissant at least 2 to 3 inches apart from the sides and each other. As a tip, use a small cosmetic spray bottle and spray a little water over the surface of the croissant dough to prevent it from forming a skin on top as they proof. Lightly cover with plastic wrap. Let proof at a bit warmer than room temperature (roughly 80°F), until it doubles or almost triples in size, 2 to 3 hours.

14. Preheat oven to 400°F. Whisk together the egg, milk, and salt to make the egg wash. Once your croissant has proofed, lightly use a pastry brush to brush a thin, even layer over the top of the croissant.

15. Bake for approximately 20 minutes until golden brown and the dough is no longer wet. Eat and enjoy! Croissants are best consumed the same day they are baked, within 6 to 8 hours. If cutting, please use a serrated knife to avoid crushing the layers.

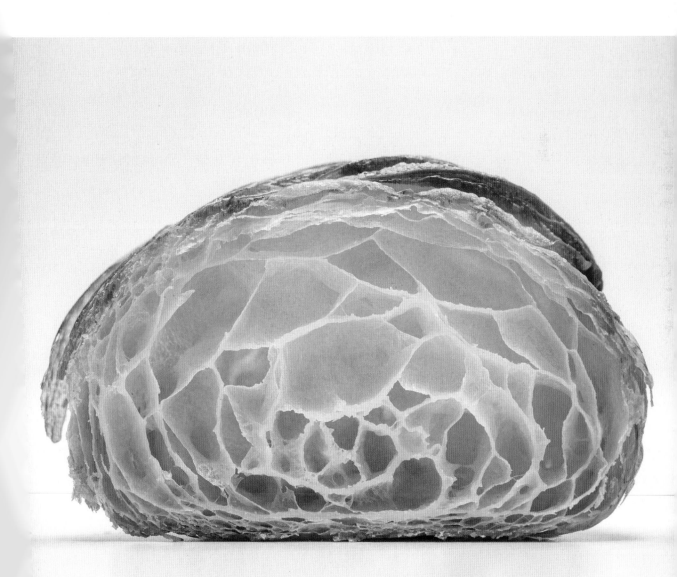

Teff Biscuits

Marcus Samuelsson's Hav & Mar restaurant in New York, NY

Makes 9 large biscuits

Active time: 25 minutes
Total time: 50 minutes

6 grams teff grains

25 grams teff flour

244 grams all-purpose flour

**275 grams cake flour, plus
more to roll out dough**

19 grams baking powder

9 grams salt

65 grams granulated sugar

**¼ pound (1 stick)
unsalted butter, cold**

**350 grams (about 1½
cups) buttermilk, cold**

¼ quart (1 cup) heavy cream, cold

Special equipment:

silicone bench scraper

Yes, this recipe mixes flour and teff—a grain from Marcus Samuelsson's native Ethiopia—into the all-purpose and cake flour mixture. But make no mistake about it, these are the southern-style, super-flaky, buttery biscuits you already know and love. They're just made even better with that nutty pop from the teff.

Whipped up in under an hour, this recipe gifts us the genius tip of grating the butter into the flour, resulting in just the right size of butter shavings without having to overwork the dough. (In the oven, those little butter shavings puff up, creating those coveted flaky layers.) Slather them up with butter, honey, and/or jam for the ultimate comfort carb.

1. Sift all dry ingredients (teff grains, teff flour, all-purpose flour, cake flour, baking powder, salt, and sugar) together into a large bowl. Grate the butter into the mix.

2. Mix butter by hand into dry ingredients. Next, make a funnel in the middle and pour in buttermilk and heavy cream. Using a silicone bench scraper, fold dry into wet ingredients until everything is well incorporated.

3. Preheat oven to 350°F. Use cake flour to flour a large, flat surface. Flip over biscuit mix onto floured surface and sift more cake flour on top of mix. Using a rolling pin, gently press down and mix your biscuit dough, rolling it into a rectangle about 1½ inches thick.

4. Using a 2¾-inch biscuit cutter (or an empty can, bench scraper, or knife), cut out your biscuits, cutting them close to one another. Place biscuits about an inch apart on a baking sheet. (Feel free to re-roll your dough to get even more biscuits!)

5. Bake 25 to 30 minutes, or until tops are lightly golden. Serve warm.

Maple Salt and Pepper Bagels

Daniela Moreira, Call Your Mother Deli in Washington, DC

Makes 12 bagels

Active time: 40 minutes
Total time: 1 day, 45 minutes

For the dough:

2 (¼-ounce) packs dry yeast

2 cups + 2 tablespoons water

¾ cup honey

2 teaspoons malt syrup

8 cups bread flour, or
high-gluten flour

⅓ cup malt powder

1½ tablespoons salt

For the boil:

6 quarts water

¼ cup malt syrup

1 teaspoon baking soda

For the topping:

½ cup maple sugar

1 tablespoon sea salt
(like Maldon style)

1½ teaspoons black pepper

Call Your Mother fans will wait a ridiculously long time for these bagels; they're just that good. And while, yeah, you'll have to wait a while too (they have to rise, after all), isn't it sort of magical that you can whip these up yourself anytime you're craving a solid salty, peppery, sweet bagel? It's up to you whether you add butter or cream cheese, or pile these hole-y goodies high with eggs and bacon.

1. For the dough, you can either mix by hand or with a stand mixer. **With a stand mixer:** In the bowl of the mixer, place yeast, water, honey, and malt syrup. Mix. Add flour, malt powder, and salt and mix with the hook attachment for about 10 minutes. Let dough rest for about 30 minutes before portioning.

By hand: In a medium to large mixing bowl, combine flour, water, yeast, honey, malt syrup, malt powder, and salt. Mix slowly until ingredients are completely combined and create a dough-like texture. On a flat surface, knead the dough for approximately 5 to 7 minutes by hand, until the dough is soft and smooth. Let dough rest for about 30 minutes before portioning.

2. To shape: Cut dough into 5-ounce portions (or 12 equal pieces if a scale is unavailable). Roll each individual piece into a small ball. Press in the center of your dough with your thumb until a hole is created. Smooth dough into a bagel-like shape and continue this process until all of your dough is shaped.

3. Sprinkle some flour on a baking sheet and place bagels on sheet (they should not touch). Cover with plastic wrap and let them sit for approximately 30 minutes, allowing the dough to rise. This proofing process must take place after the bagels are shaped.

4. After 30 minutes, place the tray of bagels in the refrigerator overnight so they can continue the fermentation process.

5. The next day, make the topping. Place maple sugar, sea salt, and pepper in a bowl and mix until well combined.

6. When ready to boil your bagels, heat water, malt syrup, and baking soda in a large pot over medium heat. Preheat oven to 500°F. Once water mixture is boiling, place bagels (no more than three or four at a time) into the pot. Boil each bagel for approximately 1 minute on each side. Remove bagels from the pot, toss on the maple salt and pepper mix (only on top) and place on a lightly oiled baking sheet to avoid sticking.

7. Bake the bagels for about 15 minutes, removing once golden brown. Let cool before slicing.

Bean and Cheese Bolillo

Arturo Enciso, Gusto Bread in Long Beach, CA

Makes 12 rolls

<u>Active time: 50 minutes</u>
<u>Total time: 5 hours, 30 minutes</u>

850 grams bread flour, roughly 7 cups

552 grams water, roughly 2 cups

2 grams (½ teaspoon) instant yeast

15 grams (1 tablespoon) salt

70 grams drained cooked beans, roughly ½ cup

70 grams (¾ cup packed) shredded cheese

toasted sesame seeds

This bread is a reimagined take on a classic Mexican roll. It's bolillo, but gussied up with pureed beans and cheese and topped with toasted sesame seeds. Arturo says the choice of beans and cheese is up to you, but he likes to stick to a creamy bean like pinto or mayocoba paired with Monterey Jack or cheddar. It's soft, crunchy, creamy, and savory all at the same time—perfect for a sandwich (torta!), but only if you can resist eating it warm straight out of the oven.

1. Mix flour and water on low speed until shaggy dough is formed, about 2 minutes. Cover and allow to rest for 15 to 20 minutes.

2. After the rest, add yeast and salt and mix on low speed for 2 minutes. Next add beans and cheese. Increase speed to medium and mix for 3 to 5 minutes, until fully incorporated.

3. Divide into 12 portions, about 130 grams each. Round and shape into an oval and let rise about 4 hours before baking. Alternatively, you can place the bulk dough in the refrigerator and shape the day you want to bake and proof for 2 hours at room temperature before baking.

4. When you're ready to bake, preheat oven to 450°F. With a sharp knife or razor, slash a line down the middle, then egg wash or spray with water and top with sesame seeds just before baking. Bake on a parchment-lined sheet pan for 15 to 25 minutes, rotating pan(s) halfway into the bake.

Sweet Potato Biscuits

Tanya Holland, chef and cookbook author

Makes 12 to 15 biscuits

Active time: 40 minutes
Total time: 4 hours, 15 minutes

1 medium orange-fleshed
sweet potato, peeled and
cut into 2-inch chunks

¾ cup cold buttermilk

2¼ cups unbleached
all-purpose flour

2 tablespoons light brown sugar

2½ teaspoons baking powder

½ teaspoon baking soda

1 teaspoon kosher salt

½ cup (1 stick) cold unsalted
butter, cut into cubes

1 tablespoon unsalted butter,
melted, for brushing

Why should you have a second biscuit recipe in your baking arsenal (see Teff Biscuits on page 59)? Because the sweet potatoes in this version from Tanya Holland give the biscuits a murmur of sweetness and somehow make the butter taste more, well, *buttery*. Be sure to plan ahead with the puree (making it the night before is ideal), and don't stress if you don't have a dedicated biscuit cutter; a glass works just as well. These are so tasty that they just might become your go-to biscuit recipe.

1. Place the sweet potato chunks in a saucepan and cover with cold water. Bring to a boil over high heat, then reduce the heat to medium and cook until very tender when pierced with the tip of a knife, about 20 minutes. Drain well.

2. Add sweet potato to the bowl of a food processor and process to a smooth puree. Measure 1 cup puree (you should have exactly 1 cup, but if not, reserve any remaining for another use). Refrigerate the puree until well chilled, at least 3 hours or preferably overnight.

3. Preheat oven to 450°F and line a rimmed baking sheet with parchment paper.

4. In a small bowl, whisk together the reserved sweet potato puree with the buttermilk. In a large bowl, whisk together the flour, brown sugar, baking powder, baking soda, and salt until well combined.

5. Sprinkle the cold butter over the flour mixture and, using a pastry blender or two table knives, cut the butter into the flour until the mixture resembles very coarse crumbs, with the butter about the size of peas.

6. Stir in the sweet potato mixture and knead it gently just until the mixture comes together and forms a soft dough; be careful not to overwork the dough or the biscuits will be tough.

7. Turn the dough out onto a floured work surface and pat it into a ½-inch-thick round. Using a 2½-inch round biscuit cutter, cut out as many biscuits as you can. Gently press the scraps together and repeat to cut out more biscuits; discard any remaining scraps.

8. Place the biscuits on the prepared baking sheet so they are barely touching. Bake until golden brown, about 15 minutes. Brush with the melted butter and serve at once.

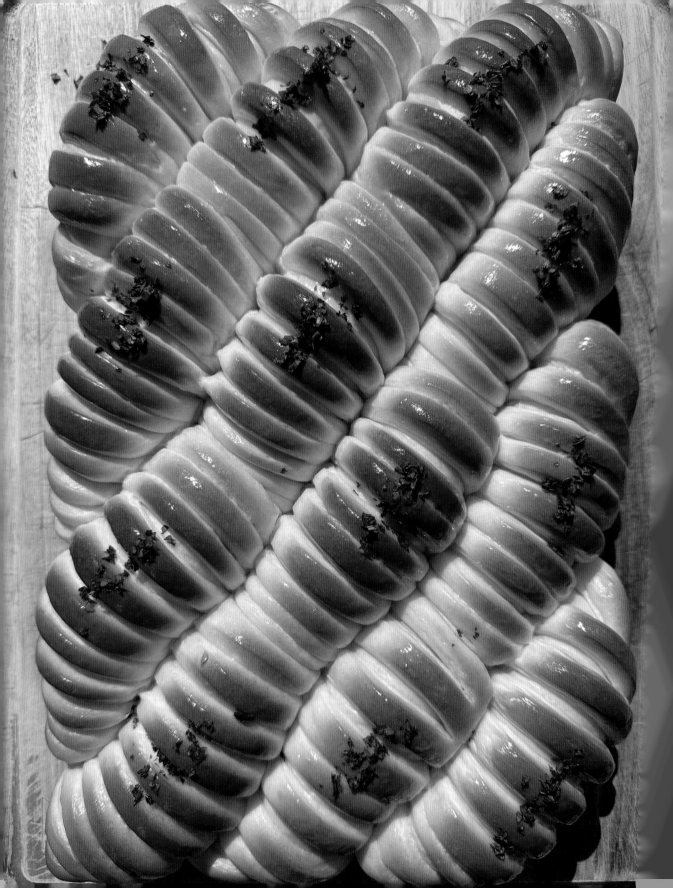

Mozzarella Stuffed Bread

Kimberly Yang, content creator (@cookim_mama)

Makes 12 cheesy bread "sticks"

Active time: 50 minutes
Total time: 3 hours, 40 minutes

For the tangzhong:

120 grams whole milk

120 grams water

40 grams bread flour

For the dough:

2 eggs

35 grams granulated sugar

580 grams bread flour

12 grams kosher salt

100 grams whole milk

6 grams instant yeast

35 grams softened
unsalted butter

4 mozzarella sticks, cut
into 3 sections (12 total)

1 egg for egg wash

1 tablespoon melted
butter, for brushing

Special equipment:

stand mixer

Sometimes you just need mozzarella cheese stuffed into your soft, slightly sweet bread. These gooey, glistening accordions get their bounce from the tangzhong (an Asian yeast bread technique that produces a softer, squishier dough, also used in the milk bread recipe on page 38) and their cheesiness from the mozzarella stick packed inside each piece. While they look impressive, the technique to achieving cheese pull heaven is actually pretty simple. You roll your dough into 9-inch ovals, then cut slits three-quarters of the way down each piece. (Use a pizza cutter or knife.) Pop in your cheese stick, roll it up, bake, and bam—mozzarella bread "sticks" are ready for devouring.

1. Make the tangzhong: Whisk all tangzhong ingredients in a small pot until no lumps remain. Then stir continuously over medium heat until the mixture resembles mashed potatoes. Remove from heat and let cool for 5 minutes.

2. In the bowl of a stand mixer, add the tangzhong and all other dough ingredients except for butter, mozzarella, and egg. Using the dough hook attachment, mix for 5 minutes until the dough comes together. Add the butter and mix for 8 to 10 minutes, or until a rough window pane is achieved. (The window pane test is when you take a small amount of dough and stretch it until the middle is thin enough to pass light through it, like a window, without tearing.)

3. Shape the dough into a ball, place into a bowl, cover, and let rise for 1½ to 2 hours, or until almost doubled in size.

4. Punch dough to deflate and divide into 12 equal sections. Form into balls. Cover and let rest for 10 minutes. Meanwhile, lightly grease a 9 x 13-inch pan.

5. Doing one at a time, roll the dough into a long oval, about 9 inches long. Cut several slits lengthwise (see process photo 1), making sure to stop three quarters of the way. Place the cheese at the end with no slits and roll into a log (see photo 2). Place into the pan. Repeat with remaining dough and cheese.

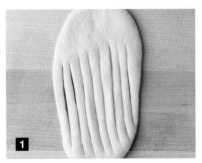

6. Cover and let rise for 30 minutes or until noticeably puffy. Preheat oven to 350°F.

7. Lightly brush your dough with egg wash before baking. Bake for 25 to 30 minutes, or until the top is golden. Brush the top with 1 tablespoon of melted butter for an extra shiny top. Tear on in!

Pretzels

Jennifer Segal, cookbook author and food blogger (*Once Upon a Chef*)

Makes 6 pretzels

<u>Active time: 30 minutes</u>
<u>Total time: 2 hours</u>

1 cup milk

5 tablespoons unsalted butter, divided

3 tablespoons light brown sugar, packed

3 cups all-purpose flour, spooned into measuring cup and leveled off

2¼ teaspoons (1 package) instant/rapid-rise yeast

1 teaspoon fine salt

¼ cup baking soda

¾ teaspoon coarse salt

<u>Special equipment:</u>

electric mixer

Maybe it's the shape that's intimidating and stops us from making pretzels at home. But really the shaping is not that hard, and this is coming from someone who can't even get people to guess the word "fish" at Pictionary. Once you get a nice, long rope of dough—you roll it, stretch it, and slap it to create a 24-inch-long snake—you simply move the dough into a U shape, twist the tips twice, and then press the ends into the bottom of the pretzel. It'll puff up a little in the oven and you'll be left with a slightly sweet, better-than-the-mall-food-court pretzel.

1. Warm the milk and 2 tablespoons of the butter in the microwave until the butter is just melted, about 90 seconds; do not boil. (Alternatively, warm the butter and milk in a small saucepan.) Add the brown sugar and stir until dissolved; set aside.

2. In the bowl of an electric mixer fitted with the paddle attachment, combine the flour, yeast, and fine salt. Mix on low speed until well combined, about 1 minute. With the mixer on low, gradually add the warm milk/butter mixture to the bowl. When the dough forms a cohesive mass, switch from the paddle attachment to the dough hook. Knead on medium-low speed until the dough is smooth but still slightly tacky, about 5 minutes. (Alternatively, the dough can be mixed and kneaded by hand.)

3. Shape the dough into a ball, place in a clean, lightly greased bowl, and cover with plastic wrap. Let rise in a warm spot until doubled in size, 1 to 2 hours.

4. Preheat the oven to 450°F. Line a large baking sheet with parchment paper and spray lightly with nonstick cooking spray.

5. In a 2-quart baking dish, combine the baking soda with 2¼ cups warm water. Stir until the baking soda is dissolved; set aside. (Dipping the pretzel dough in a baking soda solution gives the pretzels a nice golden-brown crust.)

6. Punch the dough to deflate it, then turn it out onto a clean work surface. (If the dough seems sticky, you can dust it with a bit of flour as needed.) Shape the dough into a log, then cut into 6 equal pieces; cover with a damp dish towel so the dough doesn't dry out. Roll and stretch each piece with the palms of your hands into a 24-inch rope, holding the ends and slapping the middle of the rope on the counter as you stretch.

7. Using two hands, gently dip each "rope" into the soda solution. Let any excess liquid drip off, then form the dough into a pretzel shape directly on the prepared baking sheet. Form a U-shape, then holding the ends of the

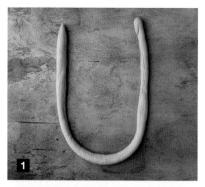

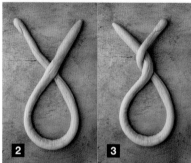

rope, cross them over and under each other—making a twist in the center—and press the ends onto the bottom of the pretzel (see shaping photos 1-4). Sprinkle evenly with the coarse salt.

8. Bake until golden, 8 to 12 minutes; watch the bottoms carefully as they can burn.

9. Melt the remaining 3 tablespoons of butter and brush on the baked pretzels. The pretzels are best enjoyed warm out of the oven or fresh on the same day (reheat in the oven or microwave).

English Muffins

Caroline Glover, Annette in Aurora, CO (adapted from Tartine Bakery)

Makes about 12 English muffins

Active time: 50 minutes
Total time: 4 hours, 50 minutes

For the levain:

20 grams starter (see page 11)

100 grams all-purpose flour

100 grams water

For the poolish:

2 grams dry instant yeast

100 grams all-purpose flour

100 grams water

For the final mix:

450 grams bread flour

50 grams whole wheat flour

300 grams warm water

7 grams salt (kosher or sea)

**semolina and rice
flours, for dusting**

Special equipment:

circle cutter

Most of us have probably never considered making our own English muffins. How would you get all the nooks and crannies? That perfect, tear-in-half-able shape? What would happen to Thomas? Caroline's recipe, adapted from Tartine Bakery, makes it remarkably easy, and the muffins are ready start-to-finish within 5 hours. You get fluffy, towering muffins with all the nooks and crannies you can slather melted butter into, and they are so good that you will eat 700 grams of flour so quickly that it could maybe indicate some self-control problems, but whatever. And don't worry about Thomas; he'll be fine.

1. Mix the starter, flour, and water for the levain in a medium bowl. In a separate bowl, mix the yeast, flour, and water for the poolish. Cover the bowls with plastic wrap and let proof in a warm space for about 2 hours.

2. In a large mixing bowl, combine the levain and poolish and add bread flour, whole wheat flour, and warm water. Mix until combined. Place the bowl in a warm spot to proof for 30 minutes, covered again in plastic wrap.

3. After that 30 minutes, sprinkle the salt evenly onto your dough and do your first set of turns and folds. (See page 18 for how to turn and fold.) Let proof for another 30 minutes. Do another round of turns and folds and then let proof again for 30 minutes. (A total of two rounds of folds.)

4. After that last 30-minute rest, dump the dough onto a heavily dusted surface with semolina and rice flours. Roll out your dough to about 1-inch thickness. Cover with kitchen towels and rest for 20 minutes.

5. Heat cast-iron or nonstick pans coated in a neutral oil over medium heat. Sprinkle more semolina flour over the top of the dough. Use a circle cutter to punch out the dough into your muffins. (Do not twist.) Cook in pan for 2 to 4 minutes on each side, until the bottom is golden brown. Place finished English muffins on a wire rack to cool. Try not to eat them all at once.

CHAPTER 3

Flats

Flour Tortillas

Ana Frias, food blogger (*Muy Delish*)

Makes 12 tortillas

Active time: 25 minutes
Total time: 50 minutes

1,000 grams all-purpose flour, plus more for dusting

1½ tablespoons table salt

½ teaspoon baking powder

200 grams vegetable shortening in butter flavor, spreadable (or lard)

2 cups hot water

2 tablespoons vegetable oil, to coat the tortilla dough balls

Special equipment:

stand mixer

comal, griddle, or large skillet

tortillera (optional)

If you're looking for the best tortilla recipe, ask a Mexican mom of nine who made them daily. Or rather, ask her daughter who grew up eating them and now continues the family's tortilla tradition. These soft little discs are worlds away from store bought, and really not that hard to make. The toughest part is in the roll, but keep rolling and turning until you get them super thin. And even if they're not perfectly thin circles, they'll still taste great and your taco will forgive you.

1. In the bowl of a stand mixer fitted with the whisk attachment, add the flour, salt, and baking powder. Whisk until well incorporated. (You can also whisk and knead by hand.)

2. Add the shortening/butter or lard and mix well until crumbly. Scrape the sides of the bowl with a spatula to incorporate all flour as you go along.

3. Change to the dough hook and turn to speed 2. Start adding the hot water little by little, about ¼ cup at a time. Mix until dough clings to the hook. Knead on speed 2 for 2 minutes longer, or until dough is smooth and elastic. (The dough should not be sticky to the touch. If it's sticky, add ½ teaspoon of flour at a time until it's no longer sticky.)

4. Place the dough in a large, oiled bowl and cover with a damp towel. Let rest 15 to 20 minutes.

5. Heat the comal, griddle, or large skillet until very hot, over medium-high heat, and then lower to medium heat before you start cooking your first tortilla.

6. Sprinkle a clean, flat surface with a little flour. Grab a handful of dough (a little larger than a golf ball), and keep the rest of your dough covered. Place dough on surface and spread with a rolling pin, from the center outward, without reaching the ends. As you roll the tortilla, turn to the fat edge and roll. Rotate the dough to give a round and thin shape. Repeat for all tortillas.

7. Making sure your skillet is hot (you should see steam coming off of it), carefully add the tortilla and cook until it starts to bubble on the edges, about 30 seconds.

8. Using your fingers or a spatula, flip the tortilla. When it starts to bubble, turn it with a paper towel, like it's a record. This ensures it cooks evenly. Cook on this side for about 50 seconds.

9. Remove from the comal, griddle, or skillet and transfer to a tortillera or a clean kitchen towel and cover.

Pita with Spicy Anchovy Oil

Alon Shaya, Pomegranate Hospitality restaurants in New Orleans, LA, and Denver, CO

Makes 8 pitas

Active time: 1 hour, 15 minutes
Total time: 7 hours, 15 minutes

1½ cups warm water

1 teaspoon instant yeast

4½ cups (540 grams) bread flour, divided, plus more as needed

2 tablespoons canola oil, plus more for your bowl and the pan

3½ teaspoons Morton kosher salt

all-purpose flour for dusting

For the anchovy oil:

¾ cup olive oil

½ teaspoon red pepper flakes, or to taste

4 anchovies, chopped

1 clove garlic, minced or grated

Special equipment:

baking stone

These are the pitas that will change your mind about everything a pita can be. Sure, they can swoosh up hummus or pack some falafel, but do not limit these spheres to swooshing and packing. These pitas can be a standalone meal, a special occasion treat, a catalyst for world peace. So pillowy you might understandably mistake them for bready balloons, they can be anything and everything, and one bite will blow apart all your preconceived pita notions. Understandably, you may be intimidated by an 18-step-long pita recipe, but don't be. It's mainly just mixing, folding, and resting, and your standalone meal, special occasion treat, and world-peace-inducing carb will be worth the time and effort.

1. Combine the water and yeast in a large mixing bowl (if you have a stand mixer, use that bowl) and let sit for 5 minutes.

2. Reserve ½ cup (60 grams) bread flour and add the remaining 4 cups to the mixing bowl along with the canola oil.

3. If you have a stand mixer, fit it with the dough hook and knead the mixture on low speed for about 3 minutes, until a sticky but cohesive dough starts to form. Pause occasionally to scrape down the bowl if the flour is clinging to the sides and bottom or climbing up the hook. If you're making the dough without a stand mixer, mix it with a wooden spoon. In either case, loosely cover the bowl with plastic wrap or a dish towel and let rest for 30 minutes.

4. With your stand mixer on low or while stirring by hand in the mixing bowl, add the salt and, over the course of 2 or 3 minutes, add the remaining ½ cup flour, 2 tablespoons at a time. The dough should be more tense; it will feel soft but tacky, although it will pull from the sides of the bowl.

5. Flour your hands generously and use them to pull the dough onto a clean, unfloured work surface. Cup your hands around the dough, rolling it in short, circular strokes and using the sides of your hands to nudge it into a relatively smooth ball.

6. Lightly wipe the inside of a large bowl with canola oil and place the dough inside, flipping it once or twice to coat. Loosely cover the bowl and let the dough rise at a warm room temperature for 1 hour.

7. After 1 hour, the dough will be stretchy but very soft. Leaving it inside the bowl, stretch opposite sides of the dough over the center. Rotate the bowl a quarter turn and stretch the dough in the same way, then flip the whole mound of dough upside down and cover again. Let rise for 1 hour.

8. Repeat this series of folds one more time, allow it to rise at room temperature for 1 hour, then tightly cover the bowl and refrigerate

overnight or up to 2 days. The longer the dough is refrigerated, the more flavor it will have. After this rise, it's ready to be shaped for pita; bear in mind that, once it's shaped, it will need more time for a final rise, so plan ahead.

9. Baking the pita: Wipe a bit of canola oil on a large baking sheet. Dump the dough onto a clean, dry counter, and use a bench scraper or sharp knife to cut it into eight equal pieces; make clean, decisive cuts rather than use a sawing motion, so you don't deflate all the air inside.

10. Lightly flour your hands and place one palm directly over the dough ball, with all your fingertips touching the counter to make a sort of "cage" around the dough. Roll it in brisk, small circles on the countertop so it tightens itself into a smoother, more taut ball.

11. Space the rounds of dough a few inches apart, seam side down, on the sheet, and roll to coat them lightly in oil. Tightly cover the sheet with plastic wrap so the dough doesn't dry out, and let them rise at room temperature for 2 to 4 more hours, until they're pillowy.

12. Meanwhile, set a baking stone on the center rack of your oven and turn on the broiler. You're emulating a 700°F wood-burning oven, so you need to give the stone a good long while to preheat before you bake.

13. While the dough rises and the baking stone preheats, make the spicy anchovy oil. In a small skillet or saucepan, combine the olive oil and red pepper flakes over medium heat. Add the anchovies and sauté until they start to "melt" into the oil. Stir in the

garlic and cook for 30 seconds or just until the garlic is fragrant. Remove from heat immediately.

14. When the dough is ready, lightly flour a work surface and use a bench scraper or thin metal spatula to coax one piece into your palm; be sure you don't manhandle it or you'll force out the pockets of air that formed while it rose. Dust a little more four on the top of the dough and onto your rolling pin.

15. With firm, even pressure, briskly roll the dough a few times along its length. Flip it upside down, rotate it a quarter turn, and roll it the same way, keeping it as round as possible.

Repeat, dusting a little extra flour as needed, until it's about 6 inches across.

16. This next part happens fast and furiously, so make sure you have no distractions—screaming children and natural disasters will have to wait. Use tongs or a good oven mitt to pull the oven rack with the baking stone partially out. Carefully pick up the pita, drape it over your palm, and slap it down onto the stone as if you're giving it a high-five (just be careful not to touch the hot stone!). Set a timer for 1 minute, and close the oven. Broilers vary in strength but all are quite hot, so don't turn your back on the oven or the pita may burn. Check on it—it should puff up and build in color, with some beautiful blistered spots. If it's still pale, close the oven and let it keep baking for 30-second intervals.

17. Use tongs to flip the pita, and let it finish baking with the oven door cracked so you can watch it finish. Pull it out when the second side is as pretty as the first; this can take anywhere from 30 seconds to 2 minutes, depending on your broiler.

18. Bake off the rest of the dough this way; as you get the hang of it, feel free to bake 2 pitas at a time. As they come out of the oven, brush or drizzle with the spicy anchovy oil. Serve hot or at room temperature.

Pizza Crust

Claire Czarnecki, Pizzeria Alberico in Boulder, CO

Makes 4 individual pizzas

Active time: 35 minutes
Total time: 1 day, 2 hours

750 grams 00 flour

431.25 grams water

23.6 grams fine sea salt

1.875 grams active dry yeast

15 grams water

While you probably don't have the 850-degree oven on hand to make exact Neapolitan-style pizza at home, you can make a very close rendition with this dough recipe. The crust is light and bubbly, with a soft, chewy center, and it will put all delivery pies to shame. It takes some planning—you need to get started a day ahead—but what's a day when pizza nirvana is involved?

1. Combine flour, the 431.25 grams of water, and salt in the bowl of a stand mixer. Using the dough hook at speed 1, mix for 6 minutes. Cover bowl with plastic wrap and let rest for 2 hours.

2. Just before the dough is ready, mix yeast and 15 grams of water to bloom yeast. Let sit for 10 minutes and then add to the dough. Mix for 10 minutes at speed 1.

3. Transfer dough to a clean, lightly oiled bowl and let rest for 30 minutes.

4. After the 30-minute rest, gently stretch one side of the dough and fold it over onto itself, rotating the dough 90 degrees and then repeating. You will lift, fold, and turn four times, until you've gone a full 360 degrees. Let rest for another 30 minutes, and then do another set of folds. Rest for another 30 minutes.

5. Divide the dough into four even pieces, about 275 grams each. Roll into balls. Place in covered bowl and refrigerate overnight.

6. The next day, take your dough out of the refrigerator at least 90 minutes before using. When ready to use, gently stretch it out to 10 to 12 inches across. Top with your favorite ingredients and bake in a pizza oven or on a pizza stone in a regular oven set to the highest heat, probably for 5 to 7 minutes, but ovens vary so keep your eye on it until you figure out your own ideal cook time.

Cheesy Naan

Barbara Javaid, content creator (@barbhomekitchen)

Makes 4 pieces

Active time: 30 minutes
Total time: 30 minutes

2 cups self-rising flour

2 tablespoons oil

2 tablespoons plain, Greek yogurt

1 teaspoon salt

¾ cup hot water

1⅓ cups mozzarella cheese, shredded

4 tablespoons butter, melted

2 cloves garlic, minced

handful fresh cilantro, chopped

Special equipment:

griddle, cast-iron skillet, or roti tawa

Finally—a speedy bread recipe! You can get your favorite Indian restaurant–quality naan in a half hour, start to finish. It's pretty much faster than ordering it. And it gets even better with the mozzarella melted into the middle that makes the already cushy bread even cushier. I use about ⅓ cup of shredded cheese per piece, but feel free to stuff it to your cheese-loving heart's content. Be sure to slather it with that garlicky, cilantro-flecked melted butter at the end for better-than-takeout bread.

1. Mix flour, oil, yogurt, salt, and water in a large bowl until combined and a soft dough ball forms.

2. Turn dough out onto a lightly floured surface and divide into four even pieces. Roll each piece into a ball.

3. Roll each ball with a rolling pin into a thin, round disc, about the length of your hand across. Place about ⅓ cup of mozzarella into the center of each disc. Gather the edges of your disc and fold up around the cheese and seal those edges. Turn over, seam side down, and roll into another disc, so you now have a thin, cheese-stuffed dough disc. Repeat for all four pieces of dough.

4. In a small bowl, mix butter, garlic, and cilantro.

5. Heat a large flat surface, like a griddle, cast-iron skillet or roti tawa, over high heat. Cook your dough until slightly puffy and starting to brown, about 1 to 2 minutes per side. Brush with melted butter, garlic, and cilantro.

Matzah

Duff Goldman, baker and cookbook author

Makes 12 to 15 matzahs

Active time: 1 hour
Total time: 1 hour, 15 minutes

3 cups all-purpose flour

2 teaspoons kosher salt,
plus extra for topping

¼ cup olive oil

1½ cups warm water

There's a lot of meaning wrapped up in this three-ingredient flatbread. (Four if you count water.) Matzah is the bread of redemption, of affliction, and of freedom. It's what Jews ate thousands of years ago when fleeing persecution in Egypt and still do, for a week straight during Passover. And while it may be intimidating to make your own bread of redemption, with Duff Goldman's recipe it's actually pretty easy to DIY it. (Just get rid of the idea of making a perfectly crisp, perfect square right now; homemade matzah is a little more artsy than store bought, but a whole lot more delicious.) You just mix, knead, roll, prick, and bake, and because it's unleavened, it's ready in a jiffy.

1. Mix all of the ingredients in a big bowl with 1½ cups warm water. Turn the dough out onto a floured surface, and knead until smooth, 10 to 12 minutes. Let the dough rest for 15 minutes.

2. Cut the dough into 12 to 15 tennis ball–size pieces. Place a baking sheet on the bottom oven rack and remove the other racks so you have room to work. Preheat the oven to 450°F.

3. Roll out the pieces of dough to about 1/16-inch thick and about a foot square. Prick the dough with a fork—make lots of holes, just like real matzah (This *is* real matzah). Sprinkle each piece with a bit of salt—just a smidge.

4. One at a time, transfer the matzah to the hot baking sheet and bake for 1½ to 2 minutes, then flip and bake for another 45 seconds. Don't overbake—you should have a good variety of color on there. Repeat with the remaining matzah.

5. As each matzah comes out of the oven, let it cool on a wire rack, and stack them only when they cool to room temperature. *Voila!* The bread of affliction!

CHAPTER 4

Sweets

Banana Bread

Snejana Andreeva, food blogger (*The Modern Nonna*)

Makes 1 loaf

Active time: 15 minutes
Total time: 1 hour, 15 minutes

3 ripe bananas

2 large eggs

½ cup sugar

1 teaspoon pure vanilla extract

¼ cup of almond milk, or any milk

pinch of salt

½ cup avocado oil, or any oil

1¼ cups all-purpose flour

1 teaspoon baking soda

handful walnuts or chocolate chips (optional)

In 2020, banana bread was Google's most searched recipe. In fact, it's ranked at or near the top of our most desperately sought-after recipes for each of the past 20 years, meaning that banana bread isn't just having a moment, it's having an entire era.

And why the heck not? Banana bread is delicious, quick to make at home, and involves fruit, so we can feel a little better about eating it for breakfast. For the best, the easiest, the don't-make-it-harder-than-it-has-to-be banana bread, *The Modern Nonna's* recipe should be on repeat. Just mash, whisk, stir, and bake, and in an hour you'll have a piping-hot loaf of banana goodness to feast upon.

1. Preheat oven to 350°F. Add your bananas to a large bowl and mash them. Add eggs, sugar, vanilla, milk, salt, and oil, and whisk it up.

2. To the same bowl, add your flour and baking soda and stir it up. If using, stir in walnuts and/or chocolate chips.

3. Pour the batter into a lined loaf pan with parchment paper and bake for 1 hour or until golden.

Somodi Kalács (Transylvanian Cinnamon Swirl Bread)

Zingerman's Bakehouse in Ann Arbor, MI, from *Zingerman's Bakehouse,* published by Chronicle Books

Makes 1 loaf

Active time: 30 minutes
Total time: 3 hours, 40 minutes

For the dough:

½ cup plus 1 tablespoon (125 grams) water, room temperature

4 egg yolks (60 grams)

2 tablespoons corn oil (25 grams)

2 tablespoons honey (40 grams)

1¾ teaspoons instant yeast (5 grams)

2⅓ cups all-purpose flour (325 grams)

¾ teaspoon sea salt

2 teaspoons ground cinnamon

⅔ cup granulated sugar (165 grams)

melted butter for brushing dough, about 3 tablespoons

For the egg wash:

1 egg

1 egg yolk

1 tablespoon water

Transylvania is a real place, and apparently it knows itself some sweet loaves. The Romanian region has made this cinnamon swirl bread for hundreds of years, bringing it out for special occasions like Christmas and Easter. It's even said that this bread was served as a wedding "cake" back in the day. But you don't need to wait for a special occasion to make this beauty, where cinnamon and sugar burrow their deliciously sweet, spicy, swirly layers into the bread.

1. In a large bowl, combine the water, egg yolks, corn oil, honey, yeast, and half of the flour. Mix with a wooden spoon until the mixture becomes a thick batter. Add the remaining flour and sea salt and mix until the dough becomes a shaggy mass. Scrape the dough out of the mixing bowl onto a clean, unfloured work surface.

2. Knead the dough for 6 to 8 minutes. Scrape down the work surface as necessary; the dough will become smooth and elastic during the kneading process.

3. Put the dough into a lightly oiled bowl and cover with plastic. Ferment the dough for 1 hour at room temperature. Combine the cinnamon and sugar in a small bowl.

4. After an hour, turn the dough out of the bowl onto a well-floured surface and use a rolling pin to roll it out to a 13-by-15-inch rectangle. Position the dough in a landscape orientation (with the long side facing you), and brush the entire surface with melted butter. Place half the total cinnamon sugar on the

buttered surface and spread it across the dough.

5. Fold the long edges at the top and bottom of the dough so that they meet along the middle of the length of the rectangle. Brush the newly exposed surface with more melted butter and about half of the remaining cinnamon sugar.

6. Grab the left side of the dough and fold it two-thirds of the way over to the right. Brush butter onto the newly exposed surface and rub half of the remaining cinnamon sugar on it. Fold the right side of the dough over to the left. Turn the dough 90 degrees counter-clockwise. Brush the surface with melted butter and spread the remaining cinnamon sugar on this surface.

7. Beginning at the side closest to you, roll the dough into a cylinder. Place the loaf with the seam side down in a 4-by-8-inch metal loaf pan that has been brushed on the inside with melted butter.

8. Make the egg wash by beating together the egg, egg yolk, and water. Brush the loaf with some of the egg wash and allow it to proof in a draft-free area for 1½ to 2 hours, or until it has risen significantly.

9. Preheat oven to 335°F. When the loaf is fully proofed, brush it with egg wash a second time and lightly score the surface with a paring knife in 3 spots to prevent air gaps. Bake for 15 minutes, then reduce the oven temperature to 320°F and bake for another 25 minutes. Using a meat thermometer, take the temperature of the loaf. Remove it from the oven at 195 to 200°F. Let cool for at least 20 minutes before removing from the pan. Remove carefully, placing it onto parchment paper or aluminum foil.

Chocolate Chip Brioche

Rebecca Eisenberg, food blogger (*The Practical Kitchen*)

Makes 1 loaf

Active time: 50 minutes
Total time: 4 hours

350 grams all-purpose flour

6 grams instant yeast

7 grams Diamond
Crystal kosher salt

150 grams whole milk (90°F)

1 large egg (room temperature)

42 grams honey

1 teaspoon vanilla bean paste

84 grams unsalted butter
(6 tablespoons), very soft
room temperature

125 grams mini chocolate chips

For the egg wash:

1 large egg

1 teaspoon whole milk

⅛ teaspoon salt

Special equipment:

stand mixer

For when you need a constellation of mini chocolate chips in your brioche, grab onto this recipe and don't let go. Seriously, it's buttery and it's chocolaty—what more could you need? You will definitely want to have a stand mixer to make this one, as incorporating all that buttery goodness into the dough takes some work, and trust me, you'd rather the machine do the work than your arms. It also takes time to get all that fat absorbed into the dough, but be patient and know that it will get there. In the end you will have a beautiful, chocolate-studded loaf ready to eat plain, with more butter, or even as the basis for the best-ever French toast.

1. Grease a 9 x 5-inch loaf pan. Combine flour, yeast, and salt in the bowl of a stand mixer fitted with a dough hook. In a separate bowl, whisk together warm milk, egg, honey, and vanilla. Pour the wet ingredients into the dry ingredients and mix on low speed until the dough comes together in a shaggy, messy ball on the dough hook, about 3 to 5 minutes. The dough will look dry at first, but will hydrate as it mixes. Be patient!

2. Increase speed to medium and knead until the dough passes the windowpane test, about 7 to 10 minutes. (For the windowpane test, tear off a grape-sized piece of dough, coat with flour, and then stretch it in the center. If it doesn't tear, you are good to go.) If the dough hasn't reached windowpane after about 7 minutes, drizzle in an additional ½ teaspoon milk while kneading, then cover and rest for 5 to 10 minutes. Knead 2 to 3 minutes more.

3. With the mixer running on medium speed, add the butter 1 tablespoon at a time. Let each piece fully incorporate before adding more. The dough will look like it is falling apart each time you add more butter, but it will come back together. Pause the mixer to gather the dough around the hook or scrape the butter down into the bowl occasionally as needed. This can take 10 to 15 minutes.

4. Increase speed to medium-high and knead until the dough is smooth, shiny, and passes the windowpane test again, about 5 minutes.

5. Plop the dough out onto a clean countertop. Press it flat with your hands, then gently stretch or roll the dough into a large square shape, about 12 x 12 inches or bigger. Don't worry about it being perfect. Just stretch it out as best you can. Sprinkle about half the mini chocolate chips on the top half of the square of dough. Then fold the bottom half up to seal the mini chocolate chips inside. You'll

now have 1 long rectangle. Sprinkle half of the remaining chips on the left half of the new clean dough surface. Fold the right side over to seal the mini chocolate chips inside, making a square of dough. Gently smush it down, then sprinkle the remaining mini chocolate chips over the new clean dough surface. Roll the dough up into a log or fold all the corners into the center and pinch them together to seal the chocolate chips inside.

6. Knead the dough briefly against the counter to help evenly distribute the mini chocolate chips inside and shape the dough into a ball. Place the dough ball in a lightly greased bowl or container. Cover and let rise 1 hour at room temperature (72°F to 75°F) until just about doubled in size.

If not doubled after an hour, let it rise an additional 30t o 60 minutes until doubled. When you push a finger into it, the indentation should fill back slowly and incompletely.

7. Turn dough out onto a clean, lightly floured work surface. Use your hands to gently deflate the dough. Stretch or roll the dough into a rectangle about an inch thick. One side of it should be about 9 inches long, the same length as your loaf pan. Fold the 2 sides in an inch or two as needed to get straight edges, then gently roll the dough up into a log. Place it in a greased 9 x 5-inch loaf pan. It may not fill out the pan just yet, and that's okay. Cover and let rise at room temperature for 1 to 2 hours, or until the dough has almost filled out the pan. When you press a

finger into the dough it should feel soft, springy, and airy, and the indentation should fill back in slowly but not completely.

8. Toward the end of the dough rising, preheat the oven to 350°F. Whisk together egg, milk, and salt to make the egg wash. Brush the top of the dough with egg wash and bake for 40 to 45 minutes, until deeply dark golden brown on top and an internal temperature of 190°F. Check the loaf after 30 minutes; if the top appears to be browning too much, tent a sheet of aluminum foil over the top.

9. Let cool slightly in the pan, then remove to a rack to finish cooling completely.

Chocolate Babka King Cake

Kelly Jacques and Samantha Weiss, Ayu Bakehouse in New Orleans, LA

Makes 2 king cakes

<u>Active time: 50 minutes</u>
<u>Total time: 9 hours, 50 minutes</u>

<u>For the dough:</u>

100 grams whole milk

2 eggs

15 grams instant yeast

550 grams all-purpose flour

110 grams sugar

6 grams salt

82 grams butter (about 6 tablespoons), room temperature

<u>For laminating:</u>

282 grams (2.5 sticks) butter, cold

<u>For the filling:</u>

475 grams Nutella

110 grams chocolate chips

<u>For the syrup:</u>

2 cups sugar

2 cups water

<u>Special equipment:</u>

stand mixer

If chocolate babka-meets croissant-meets king cake doesn't sound good to you, then why do you even have this book? This New Orleans bready dessert is so delicious that it might be one of my top 10 favorite treats. Flaky and sweet, it's a great intro to laminated dough—partly because it's totally doable and partly because the end result is just so dang tasty. The trickiest part is in the shaping, but don't stress too much about getting a perfectly round, twisty wreath. It's going to taste great no matter how it looks.

Dough:

1. Combine all of the dough ingredients except the butter in the bowl of a stand mixer. With a dough hook, mix on medium speed until the ingredients come together and start to form a ball, about 3 to 5 minutes. (If dough is too dry, add milk a teaspoon at a time.)

2. Turn the mixer to medium high speed and knead the dough, adding butter in 4 increments, allowing the previous addition to incorporate before adding the next. Continue kneading until all the butter is incorporated and the dough is homogenous.

3. Remove the dough from the bowl onto a floured work surface and form into a rectangle about 8 x 6 inches. Wrap the dough well in plastic wrap and refrigerate for 2 hours or up to overnight.

4. Meanwhile, make the butter packet for laminating: Cube the cold butter and mix in a mixer with a paddle attachment until smooth but still cold and firm. Scrape out onto one side of a piece of parchment paper and press down into a rough rectangle. Fold

the top half of the parchment back over like a book and use a rolling pin to evenly spread the butter into a 6 x 6-inch rectangle. Set aside in a cool spot.

Lamination:

5. Remove the dough from the fridge and unwrap onto a floured surface. Roll the dough into a 7 x 12-inch rectangle. Remove the butter packet from parchment and place in the center of the rectangle. Fold the 2 long edges of dough tightly over the butter so that the ends meet in the middle, completely enclosing the butter (see butter block folding photos 1 and 2 on page 103).

6. With the heel of your hand, press down along the seam, and then repeat along the rest of the dough to adhere the butter and dough together. Roll the dough to approximately 10 x 18 inches, with the seam parallel to the longer edge.

Complete a book fold: fold the two ends to meet anywhere in the middle of the dough, then fold the dough in half like a book. Rotate 90 degrees.

7. Repeat step 6, rolling the dough out in the opposite direction parallel to the folds from the previous step.

8. After 2 book folds, wrap the dough in plastic wrap and refrigerate for 4 hours or up to overnight (or freeze for up to a week).

Fill and Shape:

9. Warm the Nutella until spreadable but not hot to the touch.

10. Unwrap the dough onto a floured surface and roll out to an 18 x 18-inch square.

11. Spread the Nutella all over the dough with an offset spatula. With a knife or pizza cutter, divide the dough in half, creating a top piece and bottom piece, both 9 x 18 inches. Sprinkle the chocolate chips all over.

12. Roll up each rectangle along the 18-inch edge, creating a very tight, even roulade. Place them seam-side down and cut each roulade in half lengthwise (so it's still 18 inches long), revealing the inner layers.

13. Form the bottom two pieces into an X with the cut sides facing up. Starting at the intersection and working left, criss-cross the pieces over each other three to four times, ensuring the cut side always faces up. Leave 1 to 2 inches uncrossed at the end. Repeat with the right side. Bring one end around to meet the other and form a circle. Connect the end pieces by criss-crossing them over each other and pressing firmly to seal.

14. Repeat step 13 with the top 2 pieces. Set on parchment-lined sheet pans with at least 3 inches of space on all sides.

15. At this point, the king cakes can either be proofed and baked or wrapped and frozen for up to 1 week.

Proof and Bake:

16. Preheat your oven to 350°F. Place your king cakes in a warm spot and cover loosely with a plastic bag or wrap. Allow to rise approximately 2 to 3 hours or until almost doubled in size.

17. Meanwhile, make the syrup: Bring the water and sugar to a boil for 2 minutes, then let cool. This can be held in the refrigerator for up to a month.

18. Bake the king cakes for 40 to 50 minutes or until deeply dark brown all over. Remove from the oven and brush generously with syrup. Let cool, then share with friends (and leave the knife out—they will be coming back for more!).

Overnight Cinnamon Rolls

Kate Wood, cookbook author and food blogger (Wood & Spoon)

Makes 12 to 14 rolls

Active time: 45 minutes
Total time: 1 day, 45 minutes

For the dough:

1 cup (240 grams) milk, lukewarm

¼ cup (60 grams)
water, lukewarm

1 tablespoon active dry yeast

6 tablespoons (85 grams)
unsalted butter, melted
but not too hot

1 large egg, plus 2 egg yolks

¼ cup (50 grams) brown sugar

¼ cup (50 grams)
granulated sugar

2¾ cups (385 grams)
all-purpose flour

1½ cups (210 grams) bread flour

½ teaspoon salt

For the filling:

5 tablespoons (70 grams)
unsalted butter, melted

1 tablespoon cinnamon

1 teaspoon pumpkin
pie spice, if desired

¾ cup (150 grams) brown sugar

For the frosting:

4 ounces cream cheese,
room temperature

¼ cup (55 grams) unsalted
butter, room temperature

1 cup (115 grams)
powdered sugar

2+ tablespoons milk

Cinnamon rolls are an entire vibe. When you start your day with a gooey, cream cheese frosting–topped roll, you are setting the tone for all the giddy-inducing indulgence to come. You are setting an intention to seize that day, and all the butter, brown sugar, and cinnamon it has to offer. You are calling out to the universe, "Yeah, I know I should be eating overnight oats and doing the laundry, but I'm going to sit here and ingest half of my daily calories in under 10 minutes anyway."

But, alas, first you must plan for this kind of day. These cinnamon rolls need to sit in the fridge overnight so that all that sticky filling can marinate in its sweetness. So do the right thing today and get your dough prepped, knowing that tomorrow is a cinnamon roll vibe kind of day.

1. In the bowl of a stand mixer or a large bowl, combine the milk and water and sprinkle the yeast over top of it. Allow the yeast to dissolve, about 5 minutes. Stir in the butter, egg, egg yolks, brown sugar, and sugar until smooth.

2. In a small bowl, combine the flour, bread flour, and salt. Dump about half of the dry ingredients into the yeast mixture and stir until combined. Pour in the remaining dry ingredients and knead in the bowl using the dough hook attachment until smooth and slightly tacky, about 7 minutes. If you notice your dough isn't pulling away from the sides of the bowl or it's too wet, add flour 2 tablespoons at a time until the dough pulls away from the sides of the bowl and forms a little dough "tornado" around the dough hook. Once done kneading, place the dough into a large lightly greased bowl and cover tightly with plastic wrap to double in size, about 1½ to 2 hours.

3. Once the dough has risen, dump it out onto a lightly floured surface. Use

a rolling pin to roll it out into a large rectangle, about 11 x 21 inches in size. Pour the melted butter and spread it out over top.

4. Combine the cinnamon, pumpkin pie spice (if using), and brown sugar and sprinkle evenly over the buttered dough. Starting with one of the long ends, tightly roll the dough from end to end and pinch the edges together to seal. Cut the dough into 1½-inch sections and lay them out 2 inches apart in a lightly greased baking dish. Cover with plastic wrap and place in the fridge overnight.

5. In the morning, remove the rolls from the fridge and preheat the oven to 350°F. Keep the baking dish close to the oven while it preheats to help the rolls come to room temperature. Once preheated, bake in the oven for about 22 to 25 minutes, or until the edges are barely golden and the internal temperature is 190°F. Remove from the oven and prepare your frosting.

6. Cream the cream cheese and butter in a large bowl at medium speed until smooth, about 1 minute. Add the powdered sugar and milk and beat to combine. Add additional milk to thin out the frosting or more powdered sugar to thicken it. You can also gently warm the frosting to pour over the rolls as a glaze. Cinnamon rolls are best enjoyed warm.

RECOMMENDED READING

Want to read more from these amazing bakers and chefs? Of course you do! Here, find the cookbooks and blogs you need for more incredible recipes and inspiration.

Books

Dominique Ansel, *Everyone Can Bake* and *Dominique Ansel: The Secret Recipes,* Simon & Schuster

Tessa Arias, *The Ultimate Cookie Handbook*

Joanne Chang, *Flour* and *Flour, Too,* Chronicle Books; *Myers + Chang at Home* and *Pastry Love,* Mariner Books

Amy Emberling and Frank Carollo, *Zingerman's Bakehouse,* Chronicle Books

Duff Goldman, *Duff Bakes,* William Morrow; *Super Good Baking for Kids* and *Super Good Cookies for Kids,* HarperCollins

Tanya Holland, *Brown Sugar Kitchen,* Chronicle Books and *New Soul Cooking,* Abrams

Maurizio Leo, *The Perfect Loaf,* Clarkson Potter

Kelli Marks, *Easy One-Bowl Baking,* Rockridge Press

Deb Perelman, *Smitten Kitchen Every Day* and *Smitten Kitchen Keepers,* Knopf

Marcus Samuelsson, *Yes, Chef,* Random House; *The Rise,* Voracious; and *The Red Rooster Cookbook,* Harvest

Jeanne Sauvage, *Gluten-Free Baking for the Holidays* and *Gluten-Free Wish List,* Chronicle Books

Jennifer Segal, *Once Upon a Chef, The Cookbook,* Chronicle Books, and *Once Upon a Chef Weeknight/ Weekend,* Clarkson Potter

Alon Shaya, *Shaya,* Knopf

Kate Wood, *Her Daily Bread,* HarperOne

Blogs

Snejana Andreeva, TheModernNonna.com

Tessa Arias, HandleTheHeat.com

Rebecca Eisenberg, ThePracticalKitchen.com

Ana Frias, MuyDelish.com

Kimberlee Ho, KickAssBaker.com

Maurizio Leo, ThePerfectLoaf.com

Deb Perelman, SmittenKitchen.com

Jean Sauvage, ArtofGlutenFreeBaking.com

Jenn Segal, OnceUponAChef.com

Kate Wood, TheWoodAndSpoon.com

ACKNOWLEDGMENTS

A huge thank you to the incredible bakers and chefs who shared their recipes with me. There would be no cookbook without them, and I am so grateful to all of the kind souls who shared their bread-baking mastery with me. Thank you, thank you, thank you!

Vanessa Mir took the most amazing photographs, and I am so appreciative of her talent, patience, and calm. This book is so much more beautiful because of her.

ABOUT THE AUTHOR

Allyson Reedy is a carb-obsessed food writer and restaurant critic in Denver, Colorado. When she's not taste-testing or checking out new restaurants for a story, she's probably tripping over her pug in her home kitchen while trying out cookie recipes. Oh, and eating batter and dough by the fistful before her kids ask to lick the bowl; there's a lot of that happening, too.